ENJOY

YOURS AYE

Roger Sheppard.

A HISTORY OF THE ROYAL TOURNAMENT 1880 – 1999

THE STORY OF THE SHOW THAT ENTERTAINED GENERATIONS OF VISITORS AND RAISED MILLIONS OF POUNDS FOR ARMED FORCES CHARITIES

ROGER SHEPPARD

CW01636297

Copyright © Roger Sheppard 2025

First published in 2025 by Rare Spark

The author has asserted his moral right to be identified as the author of this work.

ISBN 978-1-0684345-0-1

Cover photographs by kind permission of Sampson Lloyd Photography
https://www.Tournamentimages.com/

FOREWORD

It's all a long time ago now, but fifteen years of my later working life was associated with The Royal Tournament, The Royal Military Tattoo of 2000 and British Military Tournament. In all cases they were wonderful ways to show to the public the versatility and skills of the three services not to mention the colourful and dynamic spectacle such a display demonstrated. Iain Ferguson, Michael Parker and Christopher Joll, the latter two now no longer with us, were the inspiration for these events and I remember fondly working, arguing and negotiating with all of them over the years but my memory registers very firmly what fun it all was.

Michael and Christopher would be so thrilled that Roger Sheppard has written this book. Roger has carefully researched the history from its early beginnings in 1880 when the beneficiary was the quaintly named Royal Cambridge Asylum for Soldiers' Widows. Since then, the event has evolved but always raising money for the Service Charities and latterly the Army Benevolent Fund, who actually arranged the event themselves. Roger worked for the Tournament in all its recent guises and so he is thus well equipped to research and write about the extraordinary story of the 120 years or so of The Royal Tournament.

Her Majesty Queen Elizabeth was a firm supporter of the Royal Tournament and came most years. We invited Her to the BMT and in 2011 she came but there was a problem. In the old set up at Earls Court there was a wonderfully arcane lift to the Royal Box but in the years between 1999 and 2010 the lift had disappeared, so Her Majesty had to scale the staircase to the Royal Box some 35 steps up! She was 85 years old at the time! She made light of it.

On the final and last performance of The Royal Tournament in 1999 the Field Gunners, who were of course the star attraction for all the years of the history, threatened to wear black armbands. I was having none of it, I delayed the second half of the performance until they were removed. Our Royal Guest was HRH The Princess Royal who, as ever, looked serene in the controversy. However, as she left Earls Court my eye lighted upon her handbag and there hanging from it was a black ribbon.

It is regrettable that with our Armed Forces getting ever smaller the luxury of laying on such a Public Relations exercise again is getting remote and so into the future the public will lose even more consciousness of their

Armed Forces. Roger Sheppard has succinctly described in this book the story of the public's interest in the Armed Forces through the medium of The Royal Tournament and those of us who held it dear should be grateful to him.

Evelyn Webb-Carter

March 2025

ACKNOWLEDGMENTS

There have been four major histories produced on this subject: Colonel Wallis King (The Tournament Book - 1911), Lieutenant Colonel P. L. Binns (The Story of the Royal Tournament - 1952), Lord Chalfont (Royal Tournament 1880-1980, A Pictorial History - 1980), and Colonel Iain Ferguson (Royal Tournament Programme 1999). All four are referenced in this book, and I am eternally grateful for the hard work of these authors in researching the history of the Royal Tournament in such great detail.

In addition, I'd also like to acknowledge the efforts of the hundreds of journalists who so diligently recorded the activities at the Tournament for more than a century. They reported in national newspapers as well as regional publications and specialist magazines, many of which are referenced in this book.

I'd like to acknowledge the efforts of the digital archivists whose work in scanning and archiving the millions of pages of newspaper print, and making them accessible for all to see, has made researching subjects such as the Tournament so much easier. These digital archives have enabled me to go further into the history of the Tournament as you will soon see. Archives which would have been so difficult to find for Col. King, Lt Col Binns, Lord Chalfont, and Col Ferguson during their respective research.

Finally, I'd like to acknowledge the generations of servicemen and servicewomen who took to the Tournament arena to entertain the public. Along with those manning the static displays, the support troops, catering teams, ushers, Police, and tech teams as well as the civilian staff over the long history of the show, all of whom helped to create the lasting legacy of the Royal Tournament.

For Claire, Elizabeth, and Harriet

CONTENTS

1 - Finale of the 1999 Royal Tournament

LIST OF IMAGES

The images in this book have been sourced from archive Tournament programmes and from Sampson Lloyd Photography. Images relating to Major Sir Micheal Parker and his artwork are used by kind permission of Lady Emma Parker. Figures 60 - 69 have been produced by the Author for inclusion in APPENDIX F – EVOLUTION OF FIELD GUN.

ONE – THE BEGINNING

The first Grand Military Tournament and Assault-at-Arms opened its doors to the public at the Agricultural Hall, Islington on Monday 21 June 1880, and so began the story of an event which would entertain millions of visitors and raise huge sums of money for Armed Forces Charities over the following 120 years.

The oldest known reference to the Tournament was published in *The Times* just 10 days earlier on Saturday 11 June 1880:

"A Military Tournament and Assault-at-Arms is to be held from 21st to 26th inst. At the Agricultural Hall, Islington. The Competitions, which are 53 in number, are to be open to all the regiments within range, and the profits are to be given in aid of the Funds of the Royal Cambridge Asylum for Soldiers' Widows. They include tilting at the ring, sword v. bayonet, lemon cutting etc. This is the first time that a general Tournament of this kind has been organized. Among the Patrons are the Prince of Wales, the Duke of Connaught, the Duke of Cambridge and Prince Edward of Saxe-Weimar. Major-General E. S. Burnaby, M.P. is the hon. Sec."

The notice stated that this was the 'first time that a general Tournament of this kind has been organized'. The Victorian public had a fascination with competitive sports, this was the era in which the Football Association (1863), Amateur Athletic Club (1866) and the Rugby Football Union (1871) were founded. Athletic Sports and Tournaments were commonplace, however the event at Islington was by far the most ambitious of its kind and it would include both regular and reserve soldiers.

In researching this book, the events which led up to June 1880 have become clearer and it's now possible to understand something of the backstory of the first Tournament and the characters behind it. When discussing the origins of the Tournament in his 1952 book 'The Story of the Royal Tournament', Lt. Col. Binns said that: "tradition insists that the idea originated with the Volunteers assembled at Wimbledon in 1878". We're now confidently able to take this timeline back slightly further with the help newspaper reports from the period.

> **Lieutenant Colonel P. L. Binns**
>
> Author of 'The Story of the Royal Tournament' published in 1952. Lt. Col. Binns served with The East Yorkshire Regiment (The Duke of York's Own) and was a member of the Royal Tournament staff from 1948 – 1963. He also published another book entitled; A Hundred Years of Military Music: The story of the Royal Military School of Music, Kneller Hall in 1959.

For two weeks each summer, the rifle ranges on Wimbledon Common were home to the annual meeting of the National Rifle Association (NRA). The NRA meetings attracted representatives from the Regular Army and from across the ranks of the Volunteers[1].

The shooting competitions at Wimbledon were one of the highlights of the Victorian Summer Season, tented villages sprung up across the Common to accommodate the participants. The various units not only competed on the ranges, but they also sought to outdo each other by decorating their temporary tented barracks, brightly coloured flower beds were not uncommon outside the regimental lines. The various messes staged lavish receptions and garden parties during the fortnight of competitions.

> **National Rifle Association (NRA)**
>
> A registered charity with a Royal Charter, the NRA's charitable objective is:
>
> "To promote and encourage marksmanship throughout the King's dominions in the interest of defence and the permanence of the volunteer and auxiliary forces, naval, military and air."
>
> The NRA was formed in 1859, and the first Wimbledon meeting followed the year after.
>
> Reference: National Rifle Association https://nra.org.uk/

It was customary for the NRA Meeting at Wimbledon to end with a Review (Parade) on the last Saturday afternoon. However, this changed in 1876. The *Lloyds Weekly Newspaper* of Sunday 23 July 1876 stated:

"It having been determined to conclude the Wimbledon meeting with an athletic meeting instead of the customary review, the management of the affair was entrusted to Mr. W. Waddell the active honorary secretary of the L.A.C., and yesterday afternoon, in the

[1] On 12 May 1859 the Secretary of State for War, Jonathan Peel issued a circular letter to Lieutenants of Counties of England, Wales, and Scotland, authorising the formation of Volunteer Rifle Corps and of Artillery Corps in defended coastal towns. These volunteer corps along with the more established Militia and Yeomanry were to provide a reserve force for the Regular Army which had become increasingly stretched during the Crimean War. Many of the modern Army Reserve (Territorial Army) Units trace their history back to the volunteer soldiers of the Victorian era.

presence of an enormous muster of spectators, and in the most brilliant weather, the sports were held. The course, which was about 700 yards in circumference, was a very uneven one. And the dry weather of the past fourtnight had rendered it anything but suitable for pedestrianism; nevertheless some good sport was afforded. The programme was most lengthy, there being no less than 28 events, about half of which were for regulars only, and the remainder for volunteers. The proceedings commenced at half-past one o'clock".

It was noted in the National Rifle Association annual review later that year:

"Athletic Sports were introduced as an experiment and instead of the Review, but it was not until the Meeting had begun that the final Programme was drawn up; consequently very little time was left to make the necessary arrangements. They are greatly indebted for the success with which attended the experiment to the exertions of Mr W. Waddell, the Honorary Secretary of the London Athletic Club who kindly placed his services at their disposal, to Major Gildea and Major Cleasby, the Inspector and Assistant Inspector of Gymnasia at Aldershot, who gave them valuable assistance, and to Captain Salmond, R.E., who undertook the arrangements of the ground".

William Waddell as the Honorary Secretary and his brother James were instrumental in the running of the London Athletic Club (LAC) during this period of its history. The Waddell brothers were sporting entrepreneurs, their LAC, a rival to the Amateur Athletic Club (AAC), attracted large numbers of spectators to events at Lillie Bridge and later to their own track at Stamford Bridge, now home to Chelsea Football Club.

Notably, the Waddell brothers staged a Grand Extra Meeting of the London Athletic Club on Monday 29 May 1876 at Lillie Bridge. The meeting was open to recognized Athletic, Football, Rowing and Cricket Clubs as well as the Volunteer Corps and Volunteer Cavalry and Yeomanry. Although not exclusive to the military, the fact that volunteer units were invited seems to indicate that the germ of the idea for the Islington Tournament of 1880 was sown at Lillie Bridge in 1876.

The competitions at the Grand Extra Meeting included:

- Four Miles Bicycle Handicap
- Tug of War (Squads of ten men)
- Bayonet Exercise for squads of twelve men

- Boxing (light weights, middle weights, and heavy weights)
- Fencing
- Single Stick
- Wrestling (Cumberland and Westmoreland)
- Horizontal Bar
- Tossing the Caber
- Throwing the Hammer
- Putting the Stone
- Long Jump
- High Jump
- Pole Jump

Duke of Cambridge

Born in 1819, Prince George was a cousin of Queen Victoria and a grandson of King George III. His military career began as a Colonel in the Hanoverian Army, in 1837 he became a brevet colonel in the British Army serving with 12th (Prince of Wales's) Royal Lancers, 8th Hussars, and 17th Lancers.

He commanded the 1st Division during the Crimean War and was present at several battles including Balaclava and Inkerman. He succeeded his father as Duke of Cambridge in 1850 and served as Commander-in-Chief of the Forces, the professional head of the British Army (equivalent to the current Chief of the General Staff) from 1856 to 1895.

Less than a fortnight later, Lillie Bridge played host to another event; a Grand Military Athletic Meeting on 9 – 10 June 1876 this time under the patronage of Her Majesty the Queen and His Royal Highness The Prince of Wales with the sanction of H.R.H. The Field Marshal Commanding-In-Chief, the latter being the Duke of Cambridge.

This event was more closely linked to Islington in that it had the backing of the Army and the Royal Family; the committee included Prince Edward of Saxe-Weimar who would later become a patron of the Islington Tournament.

It also shared a common charity with the Tournament at Islington as *The Hour* newspaper reported on 6 June that "The surplus funds will be handed over for the Benefit of the Cambridge Asylum and the Soldiers' Daughters at Hampstead" the patron of the charity being the Duke of Cambridge.

The competitions of the Grand Military Athletic Meeting at Lillie Bridge included: Tent Pegging, Tilting at the Ring, Cutting Lemons, Mounted Combats between Cavalry and Cavalry, and between Cavalry and Infantry.

The mounted competitions proved to be the highlight of the event, the *Volunteer Service Gazette* covered the meeting in great detail highlighting the competitions "between swordsmen or lancers on horseback and infantry soldiers on foot" as "by far the most interesting". The publication also suggested that these events should be linked to the NRA Meetings at Wimbledon. The hasty nature of the competitions at Wimbledon in July 1876, as mentioned earlier, would indicate that the NRA organising committee took this suggestion seriously and added the Athletic Sports in place of the Review at short notice as an experiment. As an entrepreneur and experienced promoter, William Waddell was obviously well placed to produce such an event on behalf of the NRA.

On 15 July 1876, the *Volunteer Service Gazette* published a notice stating that instead of the usual review, "The time will be, however, filled up in a most agreeable manner by a series of athletic sports and mimic combats and feats of arms, on foot and horseback, for Regulars and Volunteers, after the model of those which were so successful recently at Lillie Bridge".

The experiment of the athletic sports seemed initially to be popular. The detailed coverage of the Wimbledon Rifle Meeting the following year, the *Birmingham Daily Gazette* reported on 13 July 1877 that "Workmen are now busily engaged in the construction of the grandstand for the athletic sports. This was dispensed with last year much to the disparagement of the sight-seers". They went on to mention that the sports would include "races in marching order" as well as tent pegging, tilting at the ring and the "ordinary exhibition of athletics". The event would conclude with a tug of war between "the winners in all the military and volunteers competitions".

The following day, the *Liverpool Albion* also published a detailed report of the events at Wimbledon. They mentioned "as last year, athletic sports will be held on the common, and as this year good notice has been given to those concerned there is every prospect of a successful meeting, though in all circumstances, there was little cause for grumbling last year."

Reynolds's Newspaper reported on the Wimbledon Meeting on 22 July 1877 mentioning that the Duke of Cambridge was on hand to distribute prizes and crediting Mr Waddell again for arranging the athletic sports. They also published some of the winners of the sports; and "After a good struggle the Tug of War for the military was won by the Scots Guards, beating the famous team from the school of Gunnery".

By 1879 however, the *Volunteer Service Gazette* had 'fallen out of love' with the athletic sports at Wimbledon, hoping that an "attractive programme for the concluding Saturday" would be announced. The main concern of the writer seems to have been that there were too many competitions "in the style of the Lillie Bridge and Stamford Bridge Sports" suggesting that fewer competitions (including mounted contests and combats) would be more popular with the spectators.

On 5 June 1880 the *Folkstone Press* printed notes on the upcoming NRA meeting at Wimbledon, stating "it has been decided not to hold a review, and there will be no athletic sports, as they were not attractive enough at the former meeting to make them a financial success". A week later The Times published the announcement of the Grand Military Tournament and Assault-at-Arms. After a four-year run, the athletic sports at Wimbledon stopped in 1879, the year before the Tournament at Islington started, so the two events were never in competition with each other.

An international shooting competition was staged on the final Saturday of the NRA Meeting at Wimbledon in 1880 between teams from America and the United Kingdom. Pressure from voices such as the Volunteer Service Gazette (and undoubtedly others) likely encouraged the NRA Organising Committee to rethink the entertainment offered on the last day of the meeting and to return to their roots of competition shooting.

The jump from the Athletic Meets at Lillie Bridge in 1876 to the Athletic Sports at Wimbledon seems to be an obvious one. Particularly due to the short period of time between the three events of that year, it would appear that a series of good ideas, one after the other took the sports from the athletic track to Wimbledon Common and for a short period proved to be popular.

During the same period, a second parallel story was being played out in London, the two stories would converge in 1880.

The second story is firmly rooted in the agricultural revolution of the 19th century. From 1839 the Smithfield Shows had been staged by the Smithfield Club; they had offices in Baker Street (shared with Madame Tussaud's Waxworks). Having outgrown the space available, the Smithfield Club identified a three-acre site known as Dixon's Lairs which was regularly used as an overnight stopping off point for cattle enroute to the London livestock market.

A lease on the land was signed and the £30,000 of capital required was secured to build a "handsome, with suitable offices" – *Norfolk News* 9 June 1860. When the hall opened, it was to have at least twice as much space for the Smithfield cattle show as had been available at Baker Street. At the same time The Agricultural Hall Company was formed to oversee the build and operations, an annual fee of £1,000 would be payable to the Smithfield Club for a period of 21 years by the company.

The wrought iron barrel-vaulted roof of the main hall was 312 ft (95 m) long and had a span of 123 ft (37.5 m), at the time it was the widest span of any building anywhere. A 36 ft (11 m) wide gallery surrounded the main space offering spectacular views across the venue. The overall building was 384 ft (117 m) long by 217 ft (66 m) wide, a huge structure for its time. Construction took 18-months. Designed by architect Frederick Peck (Maidstone), built by Hill, Kedell and Robinson from Whitechapel, the Ironwork was produced by Andrew Handyside & Co, of Derby. The first Smithfield Show at the Agricultural Hall opened on Monday 8 December 1862, running until Friday of that week.

2 - Roof of the Business Design Centre (formally The Agricultural Hall) - February 2024

In the early years, the main focus of the Agricultural Hall was to stage the Smithfield Show. Other events during this period included the first Dog Show (1863) and the first Horse Show (1864), Grand Xmas Entertainment (1863), Belgian Grand Ball (1867), and Working Men's International Exhibition (1870). A Bull Fight staged at the hall in March 1870 was brought to an early close when the Secretary of the RSPCA, accompanied by several police officers, halted proceedings.

On 1 June 1876, a notice was published in *The Hour* stating that The Agricultural Auction and Agency Company Limited had "been formed for the purposes of establishing in London an auction and commission business upon a large and comprehensive scale". The notice stated that directors had obtained a lease on the Agricultural Hall for 21 years "excepting the periods in each year when the Hall is required for the well-known Horse and Cattle Shows which take place in June and December".

It appears that the Agricultural Hall was something of an untapped resource, the directors of the new company had identified the potential to stage more than just the Smithfield shows each year. The director's plan was to create a huge permanent agricultural trade show. The *Hour* also reported that the north side of the hall was earmarked for "The Agricultural Implement Department" selling all the latest equipment a farmer could need. The south side of the hall would house "The Horse Repository," fitted with stables for 200 horses. "The Carriage Bazaar" would occupy the "spacious galleries," with a hydraulic lift "under the care of experienced attendants" used to raise and lower the different types of carriage available to buy. The centre of the hall would be used for "periodic sales by auction of prize and pedigree cattle, Agricultural and Draft Horses." Further space was available in the arcade for various shops or stands selling other agricultural goods.

The directors of the new Agricultural Auction and Agency Company were listed in the notice. Among the list of directors was John Henry Raffety, the man who would become the Managing Director. His experience as an auctioneer in Wycombe and his eye for a business opportunity put Raffety in a strong position to lead the new venture.

Within a few months, the first event to be staged by the new company was announced. An advert for a Dairy Show from 24 - 27 October 1876, was placed in various publications including *Jackson's Oxford Journal*. Raffety was listed on the organising committee in September that year. He was also listed amongst the attendees of the inaugural committee meeting of the British Dairy Farmers' Association at the Dairy Show on 24 October. Later that year he was elected to the Financial Committee of the British Dairy Farmers' Association.

John Henry Raffety

John Henry Raffety was born in Wycombe, Buckinghamshire in 1842. An accident as a child led to one side of his body being paralysed, although this did not hold him back. He studied architecture and was responsible for a number of design and refurbishment projects in his hometown.

An accomplished businessman, Raffety was an auctioneer in Wycombe. He conducted sales seated on horseback in the yard of the Swan Inn. He was also the Managing Director of the first Water Company to supply fresh water to the town.

He left Wycombe in the 1870s, taking up residence in Worthing, commuting to London to work at the Agricultural Hall.

At a meeting of the British Dairy Farmers' Association the following year, on 5 February 1878, Col (later Maj-Gen) E.S. Burnaby was elected as Vice-President. The special meeting was convened to consider the proposal for the Association to take on the management of the Dairy Show themselves, entering into a similar agreement to the one in place for the cattle and horse shows organised by the Smithfield Society at the Agricultural Hall.

The attendees of this meeting (as was the norm) were published in various newspapers. The *Leicester Chronicle* places Raffety and Burnaby in the same room for the first time. Although we can only speculate on the conversation between the two men, we can say for definite that they were now acquainted.

Major-General Edwyn Sherard Burnaby

Born in 1830, he joined the Grenadier Guards and served at Inkerman and at the Siege of Sebastopol. In 1878 he was appointed Honorary Colonel of the 1st Leicestershire Rifle Volunteer Corps. Burnaby was promoted to Major-General in 1880 at the age of 50.

He also entered Parliament in 1880 as Conservative MP for North Leicestershire. As the Honorary Secretary of Grand Military Tournament and Assault-at-Arms, he was instrumental in the birth of the Tournament.

Burnaby was clearly a high-flyer, as a Colonel in the Grenadier Guards he would have been very well connected in London Society as well as his home city of Leicester. He was about to be appointed as an Honorary Colonel of the 1st Leicestershire Rifle Volunteer Corps and two years later would be elected as a Conservative Member of Parliament.

In May 1878, he was listed as presenting the prizes at the 2nd Annual sports of the Leicester Volunteer Athletic Society.

On Saturday 19 April 1879 the *Leicester Daily Mercury* reported on the opening of a new Rifle Range on land owned by Col Burnaby. He also donated the ornate silver Burnaby Shield[2] to the Leicestershire Rifle Volunteers as a prize for shooting competitions. As a keen supporter of the reserves and a regular army officer, Burnaby would have visited the NRA Meetings at Wimbledon. He would have witnessed the experiments of the Athletic Sports staged from 1876 – 1879.

The Times reported that on 29 May 1880, the Grenadier Guards under the command of Colonel E.S. Burnaby took part in The Queen's Birthday Parade (Trooping the Colour). They commented that this was likely to be his last as "after 34 years' service in the Household troops he is ripe for the Major-Generalship". As Commander-in-Chief, the Duke of Cambridge was also listed as being on parade that day. We can assume that the two men were well acquainted.

On 2 June 1880, the *York Papers* publication mentioned the newly promoted Burnaby "The annual brigade drill of the 2nd and 3rd London Rifle Volunteers took place on Saturday, under Major-General Burnaby, this probably being his last drill as colonel of the Grenadier Guards". He had been elected as the Conservative Member of Parliament for Leicestershire North in the general election of March 1880.

Raffety seemed to be the driving force behind the new events staged at the Agricultural Hall from 1876 onwards, however without a direct military connection it would have been difficult for him to obtain the support of the Army for a Tournament at Islington. The connection made between him and Burnaby at the British Dairy Farmers' Association meetings in 1878 opened the door to serious discussions with the Army and the Commander-in-Chief.

---

[2] Now housed in the museum of the Royal Leicestershire Regiment in Leicester.

When Raffety died in 1917, his obituary in the *South Buck Free* Press on 9 March 1917 mentioned many of the enterprises he had been involved in during his career including the "unique Military Tournament". It mentions that the "authorities at first opposed the idea, but it had support of H.R.H the Duke of Cambridge."

A number of publications, including the *Preston Pilot*, reported that the Duke of Cambridge attended the Athletic Sports at Wimbledon in 1877. As mentioned earlier, the Duke's charity had been the beneficiary of the Grand Military Athletic Meeting at Lillie Bridge in 1876. With these two stories converging, the stage was set for the Tournament to begin.

TWO – THE OPENING

Following the advertisement in *The Times* on 11 June 1880, other publications started to cover the story. On 12 June, the Country Gentleman correspondent of the *Sporting Gazette* wrote "Major-General Burnaby, late of the Grenadier Guards, has after infinite trouble planned a scheme which will bring a great deal of amusement not only to London Society, but to everybody who can come up to London for the week beginning June 21st". The article mentions "infinite trouble", hinting that even with the well-connected Burnaby involved, getting approval for the first Tournament had not been plane sailing. The article goes on to say that "the scheme is an enormous one, the first of the kind ever attempted on such scale in England." Assault-at-Arms had been staged in India for some years, but this was to be the first large scale event on home shores.

Suggestions were made in the press on how to improve the programme, an article in the *Daily News* on 14 June mentioned the structure of the competitions and how they would be split into four categories:

- Regular Officers
- Regular Non-Commissioned Officers (N.C.O.s) and soldiers
- Volunteer Officers
- Volunteer N.C.O.s and soldiers

They went on to suggest that the winner of each group should be entered into a fifth category to determine the overall best in that competition.

Articles also appeared in other publications that week mentioning the upcoming Tournament, including: *The Western Mail* (14 June), *The Morning Post* (15 June), *The Truth* (17 June), *The Weekly Mail* (19 June), and *The Magnet* (21 June).

Given the scale of this first Tournament, considerable planning must have taken place for weeks, if not months, leading up to the event. However, it appears that the planning meetings took place behind closed doors until the announcement on 11 June. The following week, *The Daily News* reported on a meeting of the "Patrons and Stewards of the Military Tournament" which took place at the Royal United Services Institute.

The Daily News recorded that the meeting was chaired by General Sir Charles Trollope with the objective to finalise the arrangements for the Tournament. Maj-Gen Burnaby reported on the number of entries received for the various competitions, stating that the "greatest number of entries" (48) was for the "heads and posts" competition. Other notable entries for the competitions included: tilting at the ring (45), tent-pegging (37), sword v lance (30), single stick (27), and sword v bayonet (21). Impressive numbers for the first year. A sub-committee was nominated to "settle the programme for each day," it was noted that "the more interesting competitions should be fairly apportioned over the time the Tournament is fixed to last."

The report also mentioned the discussion on the "proper method of quartering the soldiers of the line coming up from their respective regiments to take part in the competitions." It was stated that "quarters were available in the various barracks of the metropolis, or in the Agricultural Hall itself, or in the lodging-houses which surround it". It appears that at the end of the discussion it was decided that "the commanding officer of each regiment contributing competitors should be free to decide on this point." Arranging the accommodation for the competitors coming from outside London, many with horses, was probably a step too far for any Quartermaster in year one!

Perhaps the most interesting information from this meeting is related to the financial arrangements for the event. The Daily News stated that "the Agricultural Hall Company (Limited) have agreed to contribute £500[3] as a subscription to the funds of the Royal Cambridge Asylum". In previous histories of the Tournament, it was assumed that the first Tournament had not been financially successful and that the organisers had to write a cheque for the amount of £500 after the event, as this had been agreed as the minimum donation to the charity. Conversely, this reference seems to question the financial agreement in place. It appears that the £500 was a fixed amount agreed in advance of the show opening the following week. In addition, the Agricultural Hall had also agreed a further £500 towards the "prize fund of the Tournament", which the article goes on to say, "indicates their belief in the success of the enterprise".

A further article in the *Sporting Gazette* on 19 June 1880 covering the same meeting noted that the arena would be enlarged from the one used at the Horse Show (which had closed on 5 June) to "give room to rein up more

[3] Equivalent to around £51,000 in 2025

steadily". It also remarked that "all together the arrangements for the Tournament seem to be excellent."

The advertising campaign for the Tournament was gaining momentum, on 19 June an advert in *The Sportsman*, listed the Royal Patrons, mentioned the 53 competitions, highlighting a few: Tent Pegging, Cleaving the Turks Head, Tilting at the ring, etc. It also listed the number of entries for the first time - 772 in total[4]. The advert also lists the 39 regiments which would be represented along with the bands which would be appearing: "The Full Band of the Royal Engineers on Monday 21st" and the full military bands of "The Life Guards, The Royal Horse Guards, The Grenadier Guards, and the Coldstream Guards during the week".

For the whole week of the first Tournament, adverts were placed in multiple publications, stating the activities which could be seen at the Agricultural Hall "This Day". These publications included *The Times*, *The Daily Chronicle*, *The Evening Standard*, *The Daily News*, *The Echo*, and *The Sportsman*. There was a considerable amount of advertising to encourage the Victorian public to witness this new spectacle in person.

* * *

At 2pm on Monday 21st June 1880, a trumpeter from the Royal Artillery sounded the 'Assembly' and the first two combatants; Corporal Connoly, 11th Hussars, and Corporal Baker, 7th Dragoon Guards entered the arena of the Agricultural Hall. They competed in the fencing competition, with Connoly winning the first bout.

There are many newspaper accounts of the opening day, the first was printed in *The Echo* that evening "The Competitions take place in the ring, 200ft. by 80ft., the seats and stabling, as fitted up for the for the Horse Show remaining intact during the week of the Tournament". An early example of 'sweating the assets' by the organisers, utilising infrastructure for consecutive events to share costs.

3 - Fencing c. 1887 - Royal Military Tournament Booklet

[4] Many of the competitors entered multiple events. Later references go on to say that there were 112 entries in the Officers events and 660 in the Other Ranks.

The article lists all the competitions for the day and mentions "cleaving the Turk's head" and goes on to say, "representations of which have been freely distributed in the metropolis for some weeks". There are no other references to what sounds like a unique marketing campaign!

The Evening Standard of 22 June1880 remarked "Seldom has the Agricultural Hall been devoted to a better purpose than this week". The *Daily Telegraph and Courier* (along with other publications) drew comparisons with chivalrous Tournaments of the medieval days, commenting that the knights of 1880 "carried only buff padded jackets, masks, thick gloves, and foils" while the "judges wore pot-hats and long-tailed coats".

Following the fencing, the second competition of the afternoon was Sword v Bayonet (dismounted), the *Daily Telegraph and Courier* reported that with only one exception, the swordsmen were victorious saying that "the bayonet had most decidedly the worst of it".

4 - Sword v Sword (Mounted) c. 1887 - Royal Military Tournament Booklet

The next competition was Sword v Sword (mounted), the contests were between the Royal Horse Guards and members of the 5th and 7th Dragoon Guards. The participants used wooden swords covered in chalk, a successful blow being noted by the chalk mark left on the opponent. This mounted competition was popular with the crowd who cheered encouragingly as the combatants galloped towards each other!

Musical entertainment on the opening day was provided by the Band of the Royal Engineers under the direction of Bandmaster Herr J.R. Sawerthal, they played a selection from the opera 'Mignon' as the arena was setup for the next competition.

The movable platform of 30 ft square, used for the dismounted competitions was taken from the arena and thin strips of wood were placed in the thick tan laid down for the mounted competitions, at intervals around the arena to represent 'tent-pegs'. Mounted teams from the 11th Hussars and 7th Dragoon Guards entered the arena armed with lances and took turns to ride at the gallop and attempt to pick up and carry the small targets.

The 11th Hussars had recently returned from India, where the sport was popular with local troops. *The Telegraph* noted that "Over and over again the splendid men of the 11th, especially Troop Sergeant-Major Deveson – who never missed (...), picked up the peg, while the Dragoons missed, to the amusement of the crowd".

5 - Tent Pegging drawings c. 1887 - Royal Military Tournament Booklet

Further mounted competitions followed. Tilting at the ring - three rings (a few inches in diameter) were suspended on gallows at 10-yard intervals in the arena. The cavalrymen took turns at attempting to collect all three rings, one after another with their lance. Lemon Cutting – a similar setup was used for this competition, this time with soldiers using swords to slice three of the small fruits while riding at speed down the arena.

The final competition was 'Cleaving the Turk's Head', generally referred to as Head's on Post's in more modern times. In this discipline, competitors on horseback armed with swords, attempted to slice two targets mounted on metal stands (at head height), jumping a brush fence between the two, before attempting to carry away a suspended iron ring with the tip of their sword. The winner of this competition on the first day was Cpl Hunt of the 7th Dragoon Guards.

Tent Pegging

An ancient cavalry tactic, Tent Pegging is related to the idea that cavalry troops attack enemy camps on their galloping horses, using lances to remove tent pegs causing the tents to collapse, with the enemy inside.

The sport of Tent Pegging includes a similar imitation of the discipline in which a mounted horseman rides at the gallop, using a lance to pick up and carry away a small ground target, similar to a tent peg.

Reference: International Tent Pegging Federation https://itpf.net/en/

The 22 June edition of the *Sporting Chronicle* reported "Large numbers of spectators were present at both performances [on the opening day], which were highly successful". In their account of the first performance, The *Telegraph* mentioned that the reserved seats of the hall were not filled, noting "If, however, the wealthier patrons of the contest were absent their absence was made up for by the attendance of a vast number of people, who standing round the arena and occupying the gallery, took at once an enthusiastic and intellectual part in the day's proceedings".

The *Daily Chronicle* on 22 June reported on both the matinee and evening performances from the opening day, stating that the afternoon competitions took place "in the presence of a tolerably large number of spectators" while "In the evening the spectators numbered 3,000 persons". The highlight of the evening seems to have been the final of the Bayonet v Sword (dismounted) competition between Corporal McPherson and Corporal McLaren both of the Royal Horse Guards. In the second bout, McPherson (sword) disarmed McLaren (bayonet) and struck him over the head with the sabre and then taking his opponents weapon to use it against him "amid much cheering". *The Daily Chronicle* also made a brief mention of a gymnastic competition for Horizontal Bar during the evening (without much detail).

In their report on 23 June *The Daily Chronicle* commented that the competitions on the second day of the Tournament took place "in the presence of several thousands of spectators, the number present at the evening gathering being much in excess of that of the afternoon". Musical support was provided by the Band of the Royal Horse Guards (Blue) at the afternoon performance and the Band of the Grenadier Guards at the evening. *The Sporting Life* also covered the first two days of competition, even mentioning the prize money for competition winners (£3 3s) and runners up (£1 1s).

The first two days of the Tournament seemed to have gone well, press coverage was not limited to London, articles reporting on the event were found in the *York Herald, Aberdeen Journal, Bradford Daily Telegraph, Liverpool Mercury, South Wales Daily News*, and *The Scotsman*. Although not a sellout, multiple articles say that the number of visitors were in the thousands for each performance with the evening performances seeming to be busier than the matinees.

Maj-Gen Burnaby appears to have a strong rapport with the press, many of the Tuesday publications reported that he had hinted at a Royal Visit during the following day. A clever tactic, as this inevitably helped to increase the visitor numbers for the third day of competitions.

Messrs. Haywood of the Islington Bazar fitted out the Royal Box over the entrance to the Arena on the Barford Street side which had not been occupied on the first two days of competition but was about to welcome the first VIP's. *The Daily Chronicle* gave a vivid description: "The Royal Box was tastefully fitted up. From the gold cornice overhead depended rich lace curtains and scarlet drapery, looped up with blue coloured tassels, and bound with amber fringes. The floor of the box was laid with costly skins, and the back framed with flowers and foliage and lined with mirrors, that reflected a great proportion of the entire scene".

On the afternoon of Wednesday 23 June, the first Royal visitors to the Tournament arrived. The King of Greece, the Prince and Princess of Wales, and three of their children arrived at half past four (The Duke and Dutchess of Connaught joined later). The various newspaper reports of the day mentioned that both Maj-Gen Burnaby and Mr Raffety met the Royal Party and accompanied them to the Royal Box. *The Daily Chronicle* again reported on the scene: "The band of the 1st Life Guards performed selections from popular composers until the arrival of the Royal Party, when they played the National Anthem, the vast audience, which by that time filled the hall in every part, rising to their feet, and giving a hearty cheer of welcome".

A special programme was put in place for the Royal visitors (after the planned competitions had been completed), many of the officers who had already competed, returned to the arena to entertain the Royal party. The special performance brought together the most accomplished combatants from the various competition pools and included a mix of sword, lance, and bayonet combats (mounted and dismounted) concluding with tent-pegging. The Royal Party stayed until just after six o'clock when the matinee performance ended. The newspapers also mentioned that Maj-Gen Burnaby hinted at a further Royal visit on Friday.

Trade stands were a staple of the Royal Tournament in the later years, however it appears that this tradition started back in 1880, the following advert was placed by an enterprising stallholder (likely a permanent trader at the Agricultural Hall at the time) in *The Echo* on 23 June: "THE MILITARY TOURNAMENT, AGRICULTURAL HALL – Visitors can inspect J. C. HUMPHREYS' IRON TENTS, HUTS, and OFFICERS' QUARTERS – in the Gallery. FOR SALE, after 2 p.m. daily. Suit any purpose requiring Portable Buildings."

6 - Bayonet Exercise (Coldstream Guards) c. 1887 - Royal Military Tournament Booklet

The Echo also gave an account of the Thursday of the Tournament, stating "This afternoon a large and fashionable assemblage was present at the opening of the fourth day's proceedings." There were seven competitions on Thursday afternoon, including "bayonet exercise", with representatives from the Grenadier Guards, Scots Guards, Coldstream Guards, and 23rd Royal Welsh Fusiliers. The latter caused much excitement when they arrived at the Agricultural Hall on foot, in full marching order to take part in the competition.

The squad from the 2nd Battalion Coldstream Guards went on to take first prize, runners up were from the Fusiliers, however the competition was so close that these two teams were asked to repeat their drill in order that the umpire, Colonel W.S. Kenyon-Slaney, could decide on a winner.

The Royal Box was once again occupied on Friday when the Duke of Cambridge visited the Tournament. The Commander-in-Chief had given permission for the Grand Military Tournament and Assault-at-Arms to take place, and his charity was the beneficiary of the event. He was greeted with a loud cheer from the audience as he entered the Royal Box before the band played the National Anthem.

The article published in *The Referee* on Sunday 27 June said that the Tournament had "undoubtedly caught the public fancy", going on to say, "as good as the attendance of spectators has been during the week, the show this (Saturday) evening was far in advance of anything seen during the earlier days of the competition". The programme for the final evening gave an opportunity to settle the remaining competitions, including Sword v Sword (Mounted), Tent-Pegging, Tilting at the ring, Lemon Cutting, Cleaving the Turk's Head, Sword v Lance, and Lance v Lance.

Unfortunately, *The Referee* also reported that; "The band of the Royal Artillery was announced to be in attendance during the day, but to the evident disappointment of the public, they did not put in an appearance". *The Graphic* (3 July) said that the entire display concluded with a Tug of War which was stubbornly contested.

7 - Sword v Lance (Mounted), Victorian Scrapbook Image

The journalist from *The Sportsman* (unfortunately un-named) concluded his article with comments about the way that the press stand had been looked after, saying "It has been found next to impossible by those who had work to do to get standing room even in the erection supposed to be set apart for their use". This may well indicate that the press interest in the first Tournament was greater than the organisers expected.

Overall, the first Tournament seemed to have been a success. The public had turned out in good numbers, the contemporary newspaper reports spoke of the large crowds, increasing as the week went on. There were two Royal Visits, and the Cambridge Asylum was £500 better off. As with any event, there were 'improvement points' to look at in the washup meeting but the organisers must have been pleased with the outcome and the return on their efforts.

The *Sandhurst and Aldershot Military Gazette* (3 July) said: "There seems to be no doubt that the military Tournament at the Agricultural Hall last week proved a decided success".

THREE – ESTABLISHMENT

Following the initial success of the Tournament in 1880 the Duke of Cambridge gave his support for a second at the Agricultural Hall the following year. The press started to pick up the story in the spring, the *Banbury Advertiser* mentioned on 19 May that General Burnaby had "very nearly succeeded in settling all the arrangements for the military Tournament to be held again". They (along with other publications) hinted that they were "pleased to hear that the Aldershot difficulty in the matter has been also got over, [and] that the cavalry brigade in that camp will be able to attend." No further details have come to light but it would appear that there had been some sort of falling out between the Tournament organisers and the hierarchy at Aldershot. Thankfully, it had been resolved in good time before the second Tournament.

It was also mentioned that a number of foreign soldiers and officers had been invited to take part in the contests of 1881 – unfortunately, this did not come to fruition but gives an indication of how ambitious the organisers were. The *Manchester Evening News* (20 May 1881) reported on another plan of "placing the various days under the patronage of different illustrious individuals" obviously with a view of utilising the Royal Box at Islington more frequently.

On 21 May, the Royal Cambridge Asylum for Soldiers' Widows marked its 30th Anniversary at the Royal United Services Institute (RUSI) with the Duke of Connaught presiding. He said that "He was glad to know that the Military Tournament which last year produced a sum of £500, would be again held this year, and he hoped it might have an equally successful result".

The *Sporting Gazette* reported on a meeting, once again at RUSI, on Wednesday 25 May 1881 when the decision was made to hold the Tournament again. It was noted that the competitions would be spread over two weeks, 20 – 25 June for regular officers and soldiers and 27 June – 2 July for volunteer regiments. They also mentioned a point which hadn't been reported on during the previous year but had clearly 'been addressed' in the interim; "Last year there was some dissatisfaction as to the result of one or two of the competitions, but this year a very strong Acting Committee has been formed, and a recurrence of such unpleasantness is not at all likely".

8 - Lemon Cutting, Victorian Scrapbook Image

Advertising started to appear in publications such as *The Globe*, *London Evening Standard*, and *London Daily Chronicle* on 11 June 1881, the list of 'sports' included some new events; Artillery Repository Exercise, Artillery Driving Competition, and Ambulance Drill. The adverts also referred to the event as the "Second Annual Grand Military Tournament – Mounted and Dismounted Assault-at-Arms". The *Newbury Weekly News* had reported on 2 June that "So great was the success which attended the military Tournament at the Agricultural Hall last year that it is not only intended to hold another one shortly, but to make it an annual affair".

The 1881 Grand Military Tournament opened to the public on the afternoon of Monday 20 June, as mentioned above, the first six days of competition were devoted to the full-time soldiers. The afternoon opened with fencing, followed by Sword v Bayonet, tilting at the ring, lemon cutting, and Heads on Posts. The full band of the Royal Engineers (consisting of eighty musicians) providing the musical support once more.

The Echo made the first mention of another character from the history of the Tournament "The clearness and intelligibility of the proceedings were secured yesterday by the distinct enunciation of Riding-Master Dann, R.A., who announced the names of the competitors and the decision of the judges in each case".

A new addition to the 1881 Tournament was the Royal Artillery Driving Competition. Each gun team of six horses and three riders pulled their gun and limbers around a series of obstacles in the arena. The obstacles were set up as gates at 5ft 6in apart when the teams were walking or trotting and then widened to 6ft when the horses were at the gallop. The competition proved popular with the public. K Battery, Royal Horse Artillery were declared the winners in 1881.

The Royal Box at the Agricultural Hall was occupied again in 1881, firstly by the Duke & Dutchess of Teck on Friday 24 June and again on Saturday when the Prince & Princess of Wales and the Duke of Cambridge attended the afternoon performance.

The issues mentioned by the journalist from *the Sportsman* with regard to the press seats in 1880 were clearly rectified for the second year. The artist from *The Graphic* commented on 2 July 1881; "The sight is worth seeing. Mr Raffety (managing director) deserves the thanks of the Press for his kind attention; and last, but not lease, the Press seats are the best arranged it has ever been my fortune to see. If only done as well everywhere as at the Tournament, we should be better able to do our work."

Captain and Riding Master George Dann

An experienced organiser, Capt. Dann had been responsible for the annual Woolwich Garrison Games and Sports in the 1870s. He undertook the duties of Steward in the arena at the tournament for over 20 years, taking on the role at the first tournament in 1880 only standing down after the 1902 show.

George Dann enlisted in the Royal Artillery in 1849, serving as an equitation instructor at various Artillery Barracks including Woolwich, Maidstone, and Dublin. He became Riding-Master in 1859 and was commissioned as Captain 1881. His pupils included HRH The Duke of Connaught and the Imperial Prince of France. When he retired from active service in August 1888, he was the Senior Riding Master of the British Army.

Another addition in 1881 was the railway excursion, adverts were published in various regional newspapers offering trips to London to see the Grand Military Tournament on Great Western, South-Western Railway etc. showing that the Tournament was popular enough to draw an audience from outside London.

Suppliers to the Tournament were also mentioning their support in their own advertising, the following appeared in the *Western Times* on 2 July 1881 "Military Tournament, Agricultural Hall, London – The Silver Challenge Cups, tastefully and appropriately designed, which are awarded in the various contests, were manufactured by Messrs. Elkington & Co., 22 Regent Street, London".

Not all off the competitions for the regulars were settled by the end of the first week, so they were held over to the second week (which had been reserved for the volunteers). Some of the press of the day commented that the number of volunteers present were disappointing, so the addition of regular combatants would have helped to fill the programme. One of the competitions mentioned in the press during the volunteer's week was Ambulance Drill. In which, squads went through the operation of preparing a stretcher, bandaging a casualty, and carrying them off the field.

The *Leicester Daily Mercury* (4 July) reported that the Prince and Princess of Teck and their four children visited the Tournament again on the last day, military attaché from both the French and German Embassy's also attended. The report said that there were several thousand spectators at the evening performance. Publications such as the *Illustrated London News* reported that another £500 donation had been made to the Royal Cambridge Asylum for Soldiers' Widows as a result of the 1881 Tournament.

The regional press was also reporting on military Tournaments being staged in other locations around the country, including Aldershot, Dorchester, and York. These events were not yet linked to Islington, but it does illustrate that the appetite to attend such competitions was not limited to just Londoners.

During September 1881, Maj-Gen Burnaby commented in a speech at the closing dinner of the Loughborough Agricultural Show regarding the Tournament. The *Leicester Journal* recorded that the audience applauded the announcement that the charity would benefit by £500 in 1881, it also noted "Next year it was hoped to enlarge the affair, and when the public knew that their money went for so good a cause, he thought they would come more numerously than if it was a speculation on the part of the proprietor of the Agricultural Hall".

* * *

By 1882, the Tournament was becoming established. Articles began to be printed in May, publishing the dates as Monday 12 – Saturday 17 June. The experiment of extending to two weeks in 1881 was not to be repeated (yet). This year there was to be a Royal Visit on the opening day with Princess Mary Adelaide (Dutchess of Teck) opening the Tournament. Foreign Ministers were due to be invited to attend along with the Lord Mayor of London.

Adverts appeared in the various London and regional newspapers again in June, as they had done in the first two years. However, in 1882, rather than listing all the competitions and participating units, the adverts concentrated on the charity; "The Grand Military Tournament is in aid of the Royal Cambridge Asylum, which is the only institution for Soldier's Widow, who receives no pension or allowance from the Government of the Country, and who is left in old age and infirmity unprovided for". An article in the *Daily News* on 9 June mentioned that the income at the Cambridge Asylum had "proved inadequate for the intended purpose". This could have driven the change in focus for the Tournament advertising, highlighting the charity rather than the competitions.

Even at this stage, the Tournament was not a cheap event to deliver. The *Daily Telegraph & Courier (London)* mentions a figure of £3,000 which had been provided by the 'management' to cover the costs of the show (not the taxpayer), this included travel and accommodation for competitors, printing, prizes, and "The rent, decoration, and lighting of the Agricultural Hall". This is the first mention of the hire costs for the venue, and hints at a change in the financial model for this Tournament. In earlier years, the Agricultural Hall Company had been in control of the finances, underwriting the costs, and the £500 donation to the charity. The Tournament 'management' were now hiring the hall themselves, taking greater risk but potentially with greater reward. Burnaby was Vice-President of the British Dairy Farmers' Association when they did the same thing with their annual show back in 1878.The *Daily Telegraph & Courier (London)*, 9 June 1882 was the first to mention a performance to be debuted at the Tournament; "There will also be a double ride for the 1st Life Guards". Newspaper reporters were invited to see the full dress rehearsal of the display on the Saturday before the show opened. The display caught the imagination of the press, a journalist of the *Pall Mall*

9 - Cover of the Royal Military Tournament Booklet c. 1887, Musical Ride 1st Life Guards

Gazette said that "The feature of the exhibition is the ride of the 1st Life Guards, an exercise all London should see".

The *Morning Post* on 13 June, gave a vivid account of the double ride: "Next came a display which cannot fail to be considered the feature of this Tournament - the double ride or combination ride by 1st Life Guards. Thirty-six troopers entered the ring, and formed in three ranks across the western extremity, the front rank wearing spiked helmets, and being armed with lances, while the two rear ranks wore the horse-tail plume, and carried broadswords. The front rank then rode round the ring to the music of the band, then in double line, the alternative lines in reverse order went through a bewildering maze of movements in quick succession, and at length returned to form in line while the two rear ranks rode round and round, performing the most intricate movements with wonderful regularity and accuracy. Finally the lancers again rode into the centre, and then rode round and round in a circle, varying the movement by riding in the pattern of a figure 8 while similar movements were gone through by the other troopers at each end. The whole was accomplished to quick music and without a word of command being given from the commencement. This display concluded with a charge along the ring by each rank in succession, and the spectators, who during the movements had loudly expressed their pleasure, greeted the Guards on the conclusion of the performance with most hearty applause." Other publications mentioned the music played during the display included: Sir Roger de Coverley and Susan's Sunday Out.

10 - The Musical Ride of the Household Cavalry at the 1999 Royal Tournament

The Musical Ride changed the Tournament forever, it was the first true arena display (not competition) at the show. It provided an opportunity to demonstrate the expert skills and discipline of the army in an entertaining manner, setting the ground for the Tournaments to come. This display was truly groundbreaking in 1882 and is still popular today, over 140 years later, when performed by the troopers of the Household Cavalry. At the final displays on 17 June 1882, "the men wore laurels in their helmets and on their lances" the *Referee* publication reported that this was the day before the anniversary of Waterloo. They also said that the trumpet used to sound the charge at the end of the display had been carried by the regiment at the battle in 1815.

A detailed article about the Tournament in *The Sportsman* on 13 June mentions that "The arrangements are purely military (...) Soldiers stand sentinel as door keepers, and collecting tickets, while soldiers in short, are to be found everywhere. There is a military ring and precision about everything, and for the time being the aspect of the gigantic structure is entirely altered." This reinforces the point that the military were now the tenants of the Agricultural Hall running all aspects of the event themselves.

The *London Evening Standard* (13 June) Mentions the Chairman[5] of the Committee of Management as Prince Edward of Saxe-Weimar, while the "honorary secretary and manager of the sports is Major General Burnaby, M.P., the originator of the scheme".

Prince Edward of Saxe-Weimar

Born at Bushy House, Teddington in 1823, the home of his aunt Adelaide of Saxe-Meiningen and her husband the future King William IV. His father (Prince Carl Bernhard of Saxe-Weimar-Eisenach) was a distinguished soldier, having served at Waterloo.

Edward became a naturalised British subject, serving in the Grenadier Guards before going on to become G.O.C. Home District in 1870, G.O.C. Southern District in 1878, and Commander-in-Chief Ireland in 1885. He was promoted to the rank of Field Marshal in 1897, he died in London in 1902.

An article in *The Daily News* (19 June) mentioned another competition at the 1882 Tournament: "The wrestling on horseback caused considerable amusement. The competitors, attired in Jerseys and leggings, and mounted on bare-backed steeds, strive to pull one another off with one hand – no easy matter."

[5] See Appendix A – Tournament Chairmen

The popularity of the Tournament was growing again, in 1882 an estimated 20,000 visitors were in the hall on Wednesday afternoon when the Prince and Princess of Wales attended with the Duke of Cambridge. The Lord Mayor of London attend on Saturday afternoon, and Princess Mary retuned to present prizes on the Saturday evening.

By Tuesday 20 June, the *Sporting Life* was reporting that £3,000 was being donated to the charity as a result of the 1882 Tournament (three times more than the first two years combined). At the committee meeting of the Royal Cambridge Asylum for Soldiers' Widows in July 1882, General Prince Edward of Saxe-Weimer publicly thanked Maj-Gen Burnaby for his efforts in fundraising for the charity via the Tournaments. A number of publications also mention that Burnaby had taken on the organising personally and was responsible for the increase in revenue.

On 15 August 1882, *St James's Gazette* published the prospectus for the "Kensington Agricultural Hall" a proposed new London venue. It mentioned "the great success of the last military Tournaments held at the [Islington] Agricultural Hall shows the interest the public take in competitions of this kind and gives some idea of the large profits to be derived from that class of exhibition". The Tournament was clearly turning heads and was being seen as a profitable model.

* * *

The Morning Post (22 May 1883) printed the following notice: "The fourth annual military Tournament will take place at the Agricultural Hall, Islington, from June 18 to 23 next. The committee of officers to manage the Tournament is presided over by Major-General Higginson, C.B., commanding the home district. The Tournament is under the direct patronage of his Royal Highness the Duke of Cambridge, Commander-in-Chief."

Major-General Burnaby became ill during the spring of 1883. He had been unwell for some time when he travelled to the coast to take the 'sea air', visiting his aunt in Brighton. While there, his health deteriorated over the course of about three weeks, and he died on 31 May. His funeral was held at Hungarton Church (St John the Baptist) close to his family estate at Baggrave Hall, Leicestershire. The untimely loss of Maj-Gen Burnaby (the driving force behind the Tournament in the first three years) could have spelt disaster for the event. However, the first mention of a 'Committee of Management' in 1882 shows that the event was becoming more established and to some extent a succession plan had been put in place. Maj-Gen Higginson was the General Officer Commanding Home District (now London District), he was ordered to take over the organisation of the Tournament by the Duke of Cambridge himself. This appointment indicates the Duke's ongoing commitment to the Tournament.

Major-General Sir George Higginson

Born in Marlow, Buckinghamshire in 1826, he followed his father (General George Powell Higginson) into the Grenadier Guards in 1845. He saw action during the Crimean War in the battles of Alma, Balaclava, and Inkerman.

He served as Major-General Commanding the Brigade of Guards and General Officer Commanding Home District 1879–1884 and Lieutenant of the Tower of London from 1888 to 1893. In 1918 he was appointed as a Deputy Lieutenant of Buckinghamshire, celebrating his 100th Birthday in the county in 1926.

Maj-Gen Higginson was no stranger to the Tournament, as G.O.C. Home District, he had been listed as a patron of the first Tournament in 1880. Higginson appointed Colonel The Hon. Paul Methuen (who would later go on to become Field Marshal) and Capt. Thomas Tully as joint Honorary Secretary. Under the leadership of Higginson, the executive committee was made up of twenty officers. This included the Commanding Officers of the units of the Home District (Regular and Auxiliary) as well as the Inspector of Gymnasia, Aldershot, and several junior officers who had taken part in the competitions at the Tournament and could provide a competitor's point of view.

The Hon. Secretaries were installed in offices at New Buildings, Carteret Street, Queen Anne's Gate, London (close to St James's Park). Entries for the various competitions of the Tournament were to be sent to the office for their attention. Her Most Gracious Majesty Queen Victoria was also listed a patron for the first time this year, cementing the relationship between the Tournament and the Royal Family. The advertising also stated that the Tournament was 'Entirely under Military Management.'

The beneficiary charity was changed in 1883, the event was to be staged in aid of the Cambridge Fund for Old and Disabled Soldiers. The press day was repeated in 1883, on the Friday before the show opened. Members of the press were able to view the dress rehearsal of the Musical Ride by 2nd Life Guards before a luncheon where the Chairman, Maj- Gen Higginson gave a short speech about the Tournament and the new charity. Capt. Tully also spoke and confirmed that there had been over 2,000 entries (with most competitors entering multiple competitions), and that the prize fund had been increased to £600 (from £500 in previous years).

11 - Balaclava Mêlée drawing, Souvenir of the Royal Military Tournament 1901

The *Morning Post* on 19 June, described a new addition to the Tournament for 1883, The Balaclava Mêlée: "The mêlee is one of the most exciting events of the Tournament. Six horsemen armed with singlesticks, and wearing white tufts on their visors, encountered six others similarly armed, but wearing red tufts. The object of the combatants is to knock off the tufts from each other's helmets, and swift and heavy are the blows delivered for this purpose." It also recorded that the Duke of Cambridge opened the Tournament in 1883, and that the hall was close to full for the performances on the opening day.

The *Daily News* reported that the 800 boys from the Royal Naval School, Greenwich, 150 children from the Royal Caledonian Asylum, 50 children from the Guards School and Home, Westminster, as well as 40 Chelsea Pensioners were in attendance at the opening performance, all guests of the Executive Committee. The group from the Royal Caledonian Asylum were accompanied by their pipers and the Royal Naval School by their band, both paraded through the arena before taking their seats for the opening performance.

The Royal Box was full on Wednesday, guests included: the Princess of Wales (and her three daughters), the Princess of Saxe-Meiningen, the Duke of Cambridge, and the Duke and Dutchess of Teck. The party arrived in time for the Musical Ride by the 2nd Life Guards. On Thursday 21 June 1883, the *Islington Gazette* noted that the gate receipts for the first three days were double that of the previous year.

The Lord Mayor of London occupied the Royal Box on Thursday, along with representatives of foreign Embassies including France, Russia, Italy, Sweden, and Japan. The Duke and Duchess of Connaught visited on Friday, and the Duchess of Teck returned on Saturday to present prizes. Following the 1883 Tournament, the Cambridge Fund for Old and Disabled Soldiers received a donation of £2,000[6].

* * *

The *Naval & Military Gazette* reported on 31 October 1883 that Maj Gen Higginson had reconvened the executive committee, stating that a set of rules had been drawn up. It also reported that the name would be changed to the Royal Military Tournament, with the principal objective "the encouragement and development of skill in arms of all ranks of Her Majesty's Regular and Auxiliary Forces". The rules also stated that the surplus profits of each Tournament would be placed at the disposal of the Commander-in-Chief who would select the charity or charities to be the recipient of the funds. The Duke of Cambridge approved the rules of the Tournament and agreed to become President with Queen Victoria continuing as Patron.

The Victorian Army was divided into Districts for administration purposes, these were published in the Annual Army List. The 1883 list for Staff at Home[7] showed the districts as:

1. Northern District (York)
2. Eastern District (Colchester)
3. Western District (Devonport)

---

[6] Approximately £206,000 in 2025

[7] A Staff Abroad List was also published showing the overseas commands including Europe, Asia, China & Hong Kong, Australia, New Zealand, and America.

4. Southern District (Portsmouth)
5. Chatham District
6. South Eastern District (Dover)
7. Home District (Horse Guards)
8. Woolwich District
9. Aldershot District
10. North British District (Edinburgh)
11. Jersey District
12. Guernsey and Alderney District

Ireland was also separated into three districts: Dublin, Belfast, and Cork District.

From 1884, the Royal Military Tournament Committee began to offer bronze medals for District Tournaments (known as Bronze Medal Tournaments) which functioned as qualifying events for the Tournament at Islington (winners of the competitions at Islington were awarded Silver Medals). Later in the year, publications such as the *Morning Post* and *The Daily Chronicle* drew comparisons between the District Tournaments and a similar model used by the National Rifle Association to promote shooting in the regions and raising the standard of the annual competitions at Wimbledon.

On Saturday 16 February 1884, the *Army and Navy Gazette* reported on the first meeting to arrange a District Tournament in Aldershot. The report said that "Arrangements were made to hold a district Tournament, from which men will be selected to compete at the Royal Tournament in London." In April, the same publication also announced that the silver cups (previously held as challenge cups) would now be given as "the absolute property of the officers winning them in June." The winners of the district Tournaments were to have their travel expenses to London paid to compete at Islington. The pool of participants would no longer be just those within easy travel of London, now the best combatants from each district would take part.

The largest of the district events in 1884 was the Royal Irish Military Tournament staged at the Royal Dublin Society (RDS) at Ballsbridge, Dublin. The RDS has staged the annual Dublin Horse Show since 1864 and since 2007 has been the home of Leinster Rugby. An article in the *Irish Times* outlined the various competitions in 1884 (30 in total), competitors were drawn from locally based troops and the Royal Irish Constabulary., The Dublin Metropolitan Police were also included in the single stick and wrestling on horseback competitions. Bluejackets (from the Navy) and Marines were permitted to compete in the tug-of-war. There were also competitions open to boys of the Royal Hibernian Military School. The programme included a Musical Ride, and the proceeds of the Tournament were donated to Irish military charities.

Financial assistance for District Tournaments was not put in place until 1886, with the exception of Dublin, when an advance sum of £100 was obtained by the committee from Messrs. Cox & Co. (Bankers to the Royal Military Tournament). Lt. Col. Binns mentions this in his book, saying that the surplus funds from 1883 had already been handed over to the Duke of Cambridge for his charity.

The 1884 Royal Military Tournament was opened by HRH the Duke of Cambridge on Monday 16 June. Boys from the Duke of York's School, Chelsea and the Royal Naval School, Greenwich provided a guard of honour in the arena and their respective bands played the National Anthem upon the Duke's arrival in the Royal Box.

The boys from Greenwich remained in the arena and gave a display consisting of dumb-bell exercises in quick and slow time, without a word of command with accompaniment provided by their band. The ever-popular Musical Ride was performed again by the 1st Life Guards in 1884, and further displays were added between the various competitions at each performance.

An infantry display comprised of a team of men armed with bayonets against a team with swords and shields. This is likely to have been inspired by the Egyptian War which was being fought at the time. Cavalry displays were provided by the 3rd Hussars, demonstrating their bareback riding and jumping skills, and by 15th Hussars, demonstrating modern cavalry tactics. The detachment from the 15th jumped fences and fired their weapons from horseback as well as dismounted. Each rider encouraged their horse to lay flat on the floor of the arena while they fired over them, then remounted as the horse stood up again.

The Tournament programme was beginning to shift from the original series of competitions to include more displays. These were popular with the audience, who were now attending regularly in great numbers. The Tournament was still encouraging skill-at-arms but was also providing greater entertainment as well. The Tournament was also helping to bring the Army closer to the Victorian public, demonstrating the skills and professionalism of both the regulars and volunteers.

FOUR – DEVELOPMENT & CHANGE

The Tournament was now well established, and although under the management of the military with its committee, many of the press reports from 1884 acknowledged the work of John Henry Raffety. Mentioning that the idea of the Tournament originated with Raffety, the *Henley Advertiser* (21 June 1884) said that the Duke of Cambridge "expressed the opinion to Mr. Raffety that the exhibition altogether had rendered good service to the British Army". Royal visitors to the Agricultural Hall (not just for the Tournament) were becoming commonplace in the 1880s and in 1884 the hall was permitted to use the Royal prefix.

12 - Stained glass window at the Business Design Centre - February 2024

The first Tournament to be held at the newly renamed Royal Agricultural Hall opened on Monday 22 June 1885. The *Sporting Life* mentioned that the seating accommodation in the galleries of the hall had been improved this year and that: "the spectators can see from any point." They also gave an account of a new addition to the programme: "There came the great novelty of the Tournament, a combined display by Cavalry, Artillery, Royal Engineers, and Infantry".

They described the display in detail: "A fort is erected at one end of the hall, and a high wall at the other, and in the centre a river is supposed to exist. The infantry are first seen scaling the wall and advancing as skirmishers to attack the fort. They retire and make room for the Artillery, who unlimber and commence firing, and are supposed to cover the work of the Engineers, who now come in and erect a bridge over the river, which was done in the short time of five minutes and a half. The Infantry cross followed by the Artillery, the enemy's cavalry scouts are driven in, the heights of the fort are scaled, and the victory won. This display will doubtless be the talk of London, and it alone is worth the money charged for admission."

Like the first Musical Ride in 1882, the first Combined Display was another game changer for the Tournament. This piece of theatre brought the public into close contact with a military operation from the comfort of the stalls or gallery, which they had previously only read about in newspaper columns. The audience were able to witness some of the tactics which had been used operationally as well as modern weapons which were often part of the displays at Islington. The organisation of the display was entrusted to a member of the Tournament committee: Lieutenant-Colonel G.M. Onslow, who at the time was the Inspector of Gymnasia for Great Britain.

Lieutenant-Colonel G.M. Onslow

George Manners Onslow was born in 1843, the son of Lt-Col William Campbell Onslow of the 44th Native Infantry, Madras Army. He joined the Army in 1861 transferred to 20th Hussars the following year and came to England in 1867.

He retired from 20th Hussars as a Lieutenant-Colonel in 1884 and was appointed as Inspector of Gymnasia in 1885, promoted to Colonel in 1887 and in 1892 was appointed Superintendent of the Riding Establishment. He retired in 1897 and died in 1911, aged 67.

Onslow drew on the N.C.O.s under training at the Army School of Physical Training at Aldershot to provide his infantry, they were joined by Artillery, Royal Engineers and Cavalry from the Aldershot area as well. The budget for the display was £100 (equivalent to around £11,000 in 2025)[8].

The combined displays were quickly becoming the highlight of the programme and in 1887 Onslow pushed the boundaries further. The Tournament committee meeting minutes from 5 May noted (in red ink) "A new and most important addition to the Infantry display is to be an Armour Clad train with Electric Motor, rails laid down by R.E., trucks to carry Machine Guns and Infantry, this is to be kept a secret as long as possible to prevent any one else borrowing the idea". When the train rolled into the arena, the heavily armed passengers included a detachment of sailors manning a machine gun, much to the delight of the audience. This was the first appearance in a Tournament display by members of the Royal Navy.

[8] Source Bank of England Inflation calculator website

The duration of the Tournament was extended in 1888, opening on Thursday 14 June and closing on Saturday 23 June. There had been a number of reports in the press the previous year of competitions overrunning, with some bouts beginning at 10:30 a.m. behind closed doors in order to complete the programme. The first three days in 1888 were set aside for the volunteers, the second week for the regulars.

Demonstrations of physical training were popular at the Tournament right up until the last run in 1999. The first of these displays took place in 1888, there were two separate displays:

"A display of physical drill by a detachment of the Northamptonshire Regiment with and without arms" (*St James's Gazette* 15 July 1888). Two Small groups of soldiers marched into arena headed by the drum and fife band. For the first part of the display the men piled arms and divested themselves of their belts and bayonets. They conducted exercises without their weapons accompanied by music. This new form of P.T. was being introduced by Colonel Onslow when he was appointed as Inspector of Gymnasia to "benefit the soldier in wind and limb". In the second half of the display the soldiers were reunited with their weapons "using the rifle as a double handed club (...) the movements being regulated by the music."

There was also a display by the Army Gymnastic Staff from Aldershot. The display team was made up of 12 N.C.Os who performed "a series of well-executed feats on the horizontal and parallel bars" (*St James's Gazette)*.

Many of the competitions staged at the Tournament favoured the regular cavalry and volunteer yeomanry. The mounted troops were expert with sword and lance, the infantry seemed reluctant to participate in great numbers. Particularly in competitions pitching bayonets against the mounted troops (dismounted cavalry often competing with bayonets rather than infantry against their colleagues on horseback). In order to encourage more infantry competitors, the earlier Team Bayonet Drill competitions were replaced with the more 'exciting' Bayonet Team Combats in 1891.

Two teams of eight infantry (including one N.C.O.) faced each other in the arena. Each man fought his opposite number one at a time, the winner (remained standing) if they scored two hits against their opponent (who would sit down after the bout). The N.C.Os were the last to face each other. The team with the most men still standing at the end was declared the winner and progressed to the next round. The winners in 1891 came from the Royal Marine Light Infantry. This competition was popular and remained in the programme into the 1950s.

Lt. Col. G.M. Fox took over as the Inspector of Gymnasia from Col. Onslow in 1890. One of the many changes that he put in place at Aldershot (and later at other establishments) was to improve the standard of swordsmanship, increasing the number of instructors and brining in experts from Europe. As the level of fencing increased, so did the allied discipline of bayonet combat. The infantry gradually redressed the balance in the skill-at-arms contests against the Cavalry and Yeomanry.

The first overseas visitors to take part in the Tournament came from France and Australia in 1891. Four Maîtres (teachers of fencing) from the French Army gave demonstration of the French method of foil work in the arena. Volunteers from the Australian Victorian Mounted Rifles travelled from Melbourne to take part in the Tournament. They gave a display of tactical riding and jumping, mounted on horses provided by 14th Hussars. Their display demonstrated how they operated in the Australian Outback as well as quick dismounting and mounting their horses. As Volunteers they entered various Auxiliary Forces Competitions at the Tournament in 1891, picking up Silver Medals in Tilting at the Ring (Sgt McLaughlin) and Tent Pegging (Pte Mawley).

The Tournament Committee followed their own tradition to 'go-one better' added another new item to the programme in 1895: The Grand Historical Military Pageant by the 3rd (King's Own) Hussars and 2nd Battalion Buffs (East Kent Regiment). Including detachments from the two regiments dressed in uniforms from historic periods from 1572 to 1895. Under the direction on Captain Willis (Riding Master of 3rd Hussars) and Major Jackson (Buffs), The full mounted band of the 3rd Hussars led the parade, the soldiers showed elements of mounted and foot drill from the historic periods, much to the delight of the audience. The detachments from the Buffs remained in the arena as the 3rd Hussars performed their musical ride to close the display.

The Grand Historical Military Pageant was yet another first for the Tournament, to this day, regimental history is taught to new recruits to help them understand their heritage. Dramatizing military history in this way added another element of theatre to the performance, something that would be built on at the Tournament over the next 100 years.

A detachment from the Egyptian Army also took part in the 1895 Tournament, providing an enemy force for the combined display. This provided a truly international feel to the show. In his book, Lt. Col Binns noted that in 1895 that a total of 1,500 men and 300 horses took part in the show.

*   *   *

On 1 November 1895, the Duke of Cambridge was 'encouraged' to retire from the role of Commander-in-Chief, an office which he had occupied since 1856. Most records say that he was 'reluctant' to change during his time in office, although change had occurred; the practice of purchasing commissions was abolished, and the short-service system was adopted by the Army. The Duke opposed both. The structure had also been changed in 1870 so that the Commander-in-Chief was subordinate to the Secretary of State for War. His successor, Field Marshal Garnet Joseph Wolseley, 1st Viscount Wolseley, was much more open to change, and change was coming for the Tournament as well.

The position of Chairman of the Tournament Committee had been held by the G.O.C. Home District since 1883, with successive G.O.C.s taking on the role. However, in 1892, General Phillip Smith declined to accept the position on the grounds that it interfered with his military responsibilities. The committee unanimously elected General Prince Edward of Saxe-Weimar as the replacement Chair. He had been named as the Chairman of the Committee of Management in an article published by the Evening Standard in 1882 and had been closely associated with the Tournament in the intervening years, however the Prince was now in his seventies.

Wolseley continued to support the Tournament upon his appointment as Commander-in-Chief, however he dissolved the organising committee in December 1895. General Prince Edward of Saxe-Weimar resigned as Chairman. A letter from General Military Secretary Reginald Gipps to the Prince, stated that the Commander-in-Chief was "strongly of the opinion that the committee of management should be composed of officers on the Active List and on full pay". It goes on to say that "the civilian element should be, as far as practicable, dispensed with; and that the Tournament should be, as it was formerly, under the executive control of the general officer in command of the district."

The committee had grown over time and by 1895 was made up of 34 members. Many of whom were retired officers or from the Volunteers. The Tournament was rapidly becoming the 'shop window' for the Army and it made sense that the Regular Amry who made up the majority of the arena displays would want to have more control over the organisation. One of the Volunteers who was not retained by the new committee was Lieutenant Colonel Tully, who had served for 12 years. He had given the Tournament a stable footing for growth and had introduced the Bronze Medal Tournaments as preliminary qualifying competitions for Islington. He went on to serve as the Chairman of the Volunteer Tournament in 1896/7, which was staged at Crystal Palace.

Major-General Lord Methuen[9], as the G.O.C. Home District became chairman, supported by Major Crabbe, and he formed a new committee for the 1896 Tournament. One of the new members was Major Robert Baden-Powell, who would later go on to form the Scout movement. By now the Tournament was well established and was drawing continually large audiences to the Royal Agricultural Hall. The new committee stepped up and added new displays in 1896.

Approaches had been made to the Admiralty on numerous occasions to invite them to participate in the Tournament, however, it had taken until 1896 for the first Royal Naval Display to be added to the programme. Forty ratings from H.M.S. Excellent gave an exhibition of cutlass drill and gun drill. The programme notes said: "The guns are brought in and, after a short march round the arena, are cleared for action and one round is fired. Both gun wheels are shifted. The guns are then taken round the arena at the double and advance in close order, reversing twice whilst in close order, they then wheel into the centre and salute." In addition, the Naval contingent also took part in the combined display and pageant in 1896.

The Artillery Driving Competition had been popular with audiences since the 1881 Tournament, showing the skills of the gun-teams at the trot and gallop while negotiating the obstacles around the arena. This was taken a step further in 1896 with the first Musical Drive, conducted by four gun-teams from D Battery Royal Horse Artillery. Taking the practical driving skills of the teams and creating an even more popular display which would go on to entertain crowds throughout the rest of the history of the Tournament.

The pageant in 1896 was titled 'Sons of Empire' and brought representative troops to London from countries including: India, Australia, The West Indies, West Africa, and Hong Kong as well as the British Guiana Police and

---

[9] Maj-Gen Lord Methuen (as Colonel) had previously been appointed as joint Honorary Secretary with Capt. Tully in 1883

detachments from the Home Army. The final group to enter the arena were from the Royal Navy, carrying a Union Flag.

The Royal Navy returned year on year, establishing themselves as a popular addition to the Royal Military Tournament programme. Their displays

13 - Musical Drive, Souvenir of the Royal Military Tournament 1901

included drill with 9 and 12-pounder field guns as well as cutlass displays, they also demonstrated lifesaving at sea from a simulated wreck in the arena.

The Royal Navy had long been providing mobile artillery to support landing parties ashore, this role was brought into sharp focus when the Second Boer War broke out on 11 October 1899. H.M.S. Terrible was due to replace H.M.S. Powerful at the China Station, however as the situation in South Africa deteriorated, the two ships were re-routed to provide support, arriving at Durban on 29 October. They landed two 4.7-Inch guns, four 12-pounder guns, and four Maxim machine guns.

The Naval Brigade of 283 Officers and Men, along with their guns were transported inland to Ladysmith, initially by train, then by oxen and manpower. The lighter 12-pounder and Maxim guns arrived first, and it took several days for the 4.7-Inch guns, on makeshift carriages built onboard ship, to be pulled into position. Ladysmith was under siege from 2 November 1899 to 28 February 1900. The part played in relieving the siege by the Royal Navy was much celebrated, Queen Victoria sent a telegram;

"Pray express to the Naval Brigade my deep appreciation of the valuable services they have rendered with their guns."

Later that year, sailors from H.M.S. Powerful took part in the Tournament at Islington. A 4.7-Inch gun was hauled into the arena by four oxen, who were then unharnessed as the sailors moved the famous gun into position, firing one round before manhandling it out of the arena to cheers and applause from the appreciative crowd.

14 - Royal Military Tournament Souvenir Brochure 1897

Although there is no record of Queen Victoria attending the Tournament, she had been the Royal Patron since 1883. In 1897, the Tournament Committee acknowledged her Diamond Jubilee.

In 1903, the Royal Navy display, evolved from 'flat manoeuvres' on the arena floor to include the first obstacle. The programme notes for the 12-Pounder Display said: "The Guns are brought in – cleared for action – and one round fired. Both Gun wheels are then shifted; guns and limber are then dismounted and remounted. The Guns are then manoeuvred and dismounted; this time all the gear being taken to the rear. After this they are remounted and the whole battery retires. An obstacle representing a 4ft. wall is placed across the Arena, and Guns and limbers are taken over it. The Battery wheels into the centre and salutes." Competition has long been a staple part of the armed forces, it builds teamwork and leadership, it challenges individuals in controlled environments enabling quick thinking in times of crisis. Someone in the ranks of the Royal Navy was about to come up with an idea to turn this simple obstacle into an iconic spectacle. But we're not quite there yet!

The Royal Marine Artillery and Royal Marine Light Infantry had entered the tug-of-war and team bayonet competitions since the 1880s. Sailors and Marines had also taken part in the combined displays and pageants which had become the centrepiece of the Tournament during this period.

Reinforcing the point that the Navy was now a key part of the Tournament their own skill-at-arms competitions had been introduced in the disciplines of foil, sabre, and bayonet in 1894.

The partnership between the two services was cemented in 1905 when the title was changed again to the Royal Naval and Military Tournament. King Edward VII opened the newly renamed Tournament on 25 May. The pageant included 350 sailors from Chatham and Portsmouth, in period uniform from the Navy of the Elizabethan day through to the modern day (1905) Royal Navy. The centrepiece for the pageant was a 24 ft long replica of H.M.S. Victory from the Battle of Trafalgar with the famous signal "England Expects That Every Man Will Do His Duty" flying from the mastheads. The display was vast, filling the Islington Arena. The appreciative crowd once again cheered their Navy as they were reminded of the many victories at sea over the previous 350 years.

Now that the Royal Navy were a permanent part of the Tournament, the committee was reorganised again to include the Commodore's from H.M.S. Pembroke (Chatham), H.M.S. Excellent (School of Gunnery, Portsmouth), H.M.S. Victory (R.N. Barracks, Portsmouth), H.M.S. Vivid (Devonport), and the Superintendent of Physical Training, Royal Navy.

15 - Souvenir of the Royal Naval & Military Tournament 1905

By the turn of the century, there were two separate strands to the Tournament, the matinee and evening shows included more performances such as the Musical Ride and Musical Drive along with the pageants and combined displays. In addition, morning sessions had now been introduced to accommodate the competitions, thus still helping to encourage skill-at-arms. The public were able to buy a ticket to the morning sessions to watch the fencing, lemon cutting, bayonet v bayonet etc. and a full list of competitors could still be found in the printed programme. Some of finals of the more popular competitions still appeared in the afternoon and evening performances over the next few years.

As mentioned earlier, Bronze Medals were awarded to the winners of the District Tournaments, they then went on to compete at Islington for Silver Medals. In 1904, Gold Medal Competitions were added. It had been noted that many of the competitions at the Tournament had been won by the same competitors year on year. It was decided that the rules would be amended so that a winner could not enter the same competition the following year to allow others to take the title. The Rules for 1904 stated that the gold medal championship competitions were "open to all winners of first prizes in each separate event at the R.M.T since 1896 inclusive, irrespective of rank or branch of service." The journalist who suggested that an additional category should be added to the Tournament (before the first show opened in 1880) to find the overall best from regulars and auxiliaries (Officers and men) was clearly ahead of their time.

The Gold Medal Championship competitions were:

A. Foil v Foil
B. Sabre v Sabre
C. Bayonet v Bayonet
D. Sword v Sword (Mounted)
E. Sword v Lance (Mounted)
F. Tent Pegging
G. Lemon Cutting
H. Heads and Posts

The programme notes stated "This Gold Medal is similar in size and design to the Silver and Bronze Medals. The official prize list was:

1st Prize – Gold Medal and 15 guineas or 15 guinea Cup (Officers)
2nd Prize – Gold Medal and 10 guineas or 10 guinea Cup (Officers)
3rd Prize – Gold Medal and 5 guineas or 5 guinea Cup (Officers)

Another display which appeared in the 1903 programme and would have a major impact on the future of the Tournament was The Grand Military Tattoo by Massed Bands of the Brigade of Guards. The programme showed that the Tattoo took place at afternoon performances on Friday 15 May (Opening Day) and Saturdays 16 and 23 May. Although Tattoos had been performed at the Tournament as early as 1895[10], this is the first time that the Massed Bands are mentioned. The spectacle of the massed band displays at the Tournament became popular with generations of visitors.

> **tattoo** noun (pl. tattoos)
>
> 1. an evening drum or bugle signal recalling soldiers to their quarters.
> 2. a military display consisting of music, marching, and exercises. [from Dutch taptoe, shutting off of taps, signalling the closing of taverns at the end of the day].

[10] 1895 – Military Tattoo by Fifes & Drums of 1st Battalion, Middlesex Regiment

FIVE – FIRST MOVE

The Tournament had grown substantially in its first 25 years, from the early days when the programme was made up of a series of competitions, it had now become a vast piece of military theatre. The combined displays were becoming more and more innovative, and the spectacular pageants had outgrown the arena at the Royal Agricultural Hall. The number of participants had also grown over the years. There were stories of soldiers preferring to sleep in the public seating areas once the crowds had left for the evening, in preference over the overcrowded temporary tented barracks which were set up in the galleries at the Royal Agricultural Hall. There had long been suggestions that the Tournament would be better placed in fashionable West London, which was more accessible on the railway network. There had also been mentions in the press that the audience numbers had been on the decline, and that the programme was becoming repetitive (except for the pageant, which had a new theme each year).

As mentioned earlier, the proposal to build the 'Kensington Agricultural Hall' was first raised in 1882. Shortly before his death in 1883, Maj-Gen Burnaby was linked to the project. The *Northwich Guardian* reported on 25 April 1883, "A company is being formed for the erection, near Addison Road Station [...] of an agricultural hall, which is to be half as large again as that at Islington. The buildings will include a central hall about 400 feet long, to be used for agricultural and trade exhibitions, Tournaments, and concerts on a large scale", it went on to say that "Major-General Burnaby is one of the principal promoters." The following year, the *Grantham Journal* remarked on 17 May 1884 that "the late Major-General Burnaby, M.P., devoted the greater proportion of the last year of his life to the furtherance and development of the scheme."

The National Agricultural Hall Company Limited was formed in May 1884 with £200,000 of capital (20,000 shares at £10 each). The foundation stone was laid in July 1885 and the building opened in December 1886. The first show at the venue was the Paris Hippodrome, a huge circus including Olympian races, Arabian horses, Roman wrestling, and Chariot racing. It was performed for the first time outside Paris. Before the building opened to the public, it became known as Olympia.

The larger venue of Olympia would be able to accommodate bigger audiences and provide more space for the performers, their horses, and equipment. However, there were some concerned voices from within the Tournament organising committee, and the press. The Tournament had a strong local following in Islington (it had been home to the show since its inception), would spectators travel to the new venue, would the West London audience be interested in such a performance? Was the new venue too big? The audience at Islington had been so close to the action at the Agricultural Hall, would that be lost on the bigger stage? And of course, would it be financially viable? Burnaby was something of a visionary; he'd been planning this move within a few years of the first Tournament. Now, over 20 years after his death, it was coming to fruition.

16 - The Royal Naval & Military Tournament Programme 1907

The first Tournament opened at Olympia on 17 May 1906. The programme included many favourites from Islington: the Musical Drive, Display of Field Gun Drill, Musical Ride, and the Artillery Driving Competition. The Navy also gave a display entitled 'Crossing the Line', described in the press as something of a 'pantomime' with characters dressed as Neptune and his staff enacting the ceremony carried out when a ship crosses the equator.

During the early years at Islington, the press often drew comparisons with medieval chivalric Tournaments found in historic texts. This was brought to life in the arena at Olympia in 1906 with a pageant titled 'Tilting in the Tudor Times'. The Edwardian cavalrymen playing the part of the knights of old aimed to unseat their opponent using their lance. The whole scene was recreated, with Lords and Ladies present in the arena dressed in vibrant costumes. The Military Theatre of the Tournament had now arrived in fashionable Kensington. The records show that there was no charitable donation made following the last Islington Tournament in 1905, the donation from the first Olympia show in 1906 was £8,000. The decision to relocate had proved successful and the Tournament was once again on a positive footing.

* * *

The Royal Navy had been conducting displays of Field Gun Drill at the Tournament since 1896 often demonstrating how they transported their guns over obstacles. These included narrow bridges and walls. This took a huge step forward in 1907 with the introduction of the Naval Field Gun Competition. The competition would go on to become synonymous with the Tournament. Even today, it is often identified as the point of difference between the show and other events such as the Royal Edinburgh Military Tattoo or Aldershot Tattoo for example. We have devoted two appendices to the subject, one covering the evolution of the competition and another logging the winners of the various cups from 1907 to 1999.

17 - H.M.S. Cambridge, winners of the first Field Gun Competition in 1907

The first competition in 1907 was very different to the one which would become familiar to later audiences. However, what it did have in common is that it was a 'competition.' This harked back to the origins of the Tournament and those early combats and team competitions. The 'competition' was always at the heart of Field Gun. Generations of Field Gunners had one single thing in common, their desire to WIN was unwavering.

The Royal Navy Field Gun Competition was established in 1907 when the first trophy was awarded. Six crews competed from the Naval Barracks and Gunnery Schools at Portsmouth, Devonport, and the Nore (Chatham). Two crews competed at each afternoon performance. The first obstacle encountered by each crew was a set of planks (3 ft wide) at a height of 18 inches off the ground, the gun, limber, and crew had to pass underneath. The next obstacle was a 5 ft wall, which the crew, gun, and limber passed over. Each gun was brought into action, the muzzle being passed through a hole in a board before firing. The crews then returned to the start/finish line passing over and under the obstacles as before.

The first crew to cross the line (providing that no rules had been broken) was awarded one point. The crew with the most points at the end of the Tournament was awarded the trophy. The first winners were H.M.S. Cambridge (Devonport). This new competition proved to be popular with the audience and became part of the Tournament programme right up until the end.

* * *

The evening performances in 1907 included a Military Tattoo and Torchlight Procession. Similar displays had occurred in earlier Tournaments on occasion but were not a daily occurrence. The pageant in 1907 was an evolution of the previous year titled 'The Tournament in the Olden Days'. A medieval castle wall was erected at one end of the arena which was filled with activity including bouts with quarter staff, archers, and boys playing leapfrog. The Queen of the Tournament was seen on the battlements of the castle, accompanied by trumpeters and her ladies-in-waiting before entering the arena to witness the combats first hand and present the prizes to the winners.

The press commented that this pageant was spectacular, although it had been produced at short notice. The original plan to reenact the Attack on Delhi Gate from the Indian Mutiny had not been 'approved' for the show.

The decision was taken to build on the success of the Pageant from the previous year and it paid off as the audience and press both enjoyed it. Physical Training was once again a popular feature with the Royal Naval School of Physical Training providing a display of the 'Swedish System' in 1907.

Overseas visitors once again took part in the 1908 Tournament, with a detachment from the West African Regiment travelling to London to take part. They provided two displays. A Native War Dance display including an African King accompanied by his prime minister, wives, medicine men, warriors, and a prisoner (according to the programme, the prisoner was sentenced to death at each performance). They also demonstrated a Bush Fight, a column of West African Troops demonstrating how they advance on foot using narrow bush paths before being ambushed by an enemy which they outflank and eventually overcome. Overseas performers such as this were hugely popular with the press and the public. Giving an opportunity to see troops from across the Empire first hand.

At each performance of the 1909 Tournament, audiences witnessed a representation of the landing of 'a force of all arms despatched from England to re-enforce the garrison of a Colony' in a display titled "Transporting Troops to a Theatre of War". A detailed plan in the programme enabled the audience to make sense of the various areas from disembarkation onto the beach, tented accommodation with cooking facilities through to a signal station and defences as well as a bridge crossing a 'notional stream.' In the same year a display of 'Hedge Row Fighting; was given by two detachments of the 25th (County of London) Cyclist Battalion, The London Regiment. However, it appears that Hedge Rows were in short supply, the programme notes opened with "The Spectators will kindly imagine that the arena represents a track of country intersected by a long road with hedges on either side, with cross roads, etc."

* * *

In April 1911 'The Tournament Book' was published by Gale & Polden, with the sub-title 'Being the Story of the Royal Naval & Military Tournament: what it has done, and is doing, to promote Skill-at-Arms and to help Service Charities'. It was issued to commemorate the Coronation of King George V, the 'Tournament's Most Gracious Patron.' It was written by Colonel (later Brigadier-General) Wallis King, Honorary Secretary of the Royal Naval & Military Tournament.

The book was written as a means of promoting the upcoming Tournament following the difficult circumstances surrounding the previous year's show.

Advertising had begun as usual in the spring for the 1910 Royal Naval and Military Tournament, which was due to open at Olympia on 16 May. The organisers of the Tournament were getting ready to move from their offices at 66 Victoria St. to temporary accommodation at Olympia ready for the setup of the show when the news broke of the death of King Edward VII, who had died at Buckingham Palace late on Friday 6 May. As Prince of Wales and later King Edward VII, he had been a patron of the Tournament throughout its 30-year history to this point.

Brigadier-General Sir Charles Wallis King

Captain C.W. King of the Army Service Corps first became involved with the Tournament in 1897, when he took on the role of Assistant Honorary Treasurer, taking over fully as the Hon. Treasurer in 1900.

In 1911 he was appointed as Hon. Secretary and Manager. As the Manager, he was responsible for overseeing the administration and delivery of each Tournament, working with a small permanent staff to plan the logistics and content of the performance each year. He stood down as Hon. Secretary and Manager in 1934 handing over to his son, Captain C.W.C King, Royal Army Service Corps.

During the period that he was involved in the Tournament, it had evolved from a series of skill-at-arms competition to the impressive military pageants of the 1930s. Having retired from the Army in 1919, he was able to concentrate on the development of the show in the inter-war years.

Announcing his death in 1943, The *Yorkshire Post* referred to Brig. Gen, King as a "Tournament Builder", he had been involved with the show for more than 40 years.

As the Nation went in to mourning, the Tournament was put on hold. With a State Funeral planned for 20 May, articles started appearing in various publications on 12 May, stating that the plans for the Naval and Military Tournament had been abandoned "by order of the War Office". The *London Evening Standard* said that a sum of Ten Thousand Pounds had already been committed to the show prior to its cancellation. A plan had also been mentioned in the press of a revised performance going ahead on the dates which had been publicised, except for the day of the funeral itself – this did not come to fruition.

It had already been a turbulent year for the Tournament, with Hon. Sec. Colonel Ricardo resigning in April over the proposed pageant 'The Millenium' which did not meet with the approval of the War Office. The proposed pageant would have seen troops singing an 'Ode to Peace.' Col. Nugent (Irish Guards) was appointed as replacement Hon. Sec shortly before the Tournament was due to open.

It was announced on 28 May that the new King, George V had approved that the Tournament would go ahead at Olympia from 20 June to 6 July. In his book, Col. King said that the previous losses had been wiped and that enough money had been brought in by the rescheduled 1910 Tournament to secure the Tournament for the next year without drawing on the reserve fund.

*   *   *

Under the guidance of Col. Nugent, the content of the pageant of 1910 was reworked (and approved by the War Office) in time for the revised dates; Britannia's Muster had a cast of 400 and included 175 horses, the display was accompanied by the full band of the Coldstream Guards. Upon entering the arena, Britannia summed the home troops first with representatives from the Navy and Army including the newly created Territorial Force[11] as well as the Boy Scouts[12]. She then summoned troops from her Colonies including South Africa, Australia, New Zealand, Canada, and India. Within a few short years, these troops would be side by side on the battlefield.

The patriotic theme continued in 1911 with a pageant entitled 'Heroes of British History' with troops entering the arena depicting characters such as Alfred the Great, King Harold, William the Conqueror, Robert the Bruce, Henry V, Henry VIII, and Sir Francis Drake. The groups formed two tableau, the first in historical order in front of the Royal Box. In the second, the groups formed a 'hollow square' in the centre of the arena, where the historic characters were joined by their 'modern day' successors from the Royal Navy and Army. Another large affair, the programme notes state that there were 320 men and 100 horses in the 1911 pageant.

The following year (1912), the Historical Episode (as the committee preferred to call it) was 'The Call to Arms, 1588', which included two separate scenes. The first represented the famous game of Bowls on

---

[11] Created on 1 April 1908 following the Territorial and Reserves Forces Act, 1907 as part of the reforms to the Army by Secretary of State Richard Burdon Haldane.

[12] The Boy Scout movement was founded in 1908 by Lieutenant General Robert (later Lord) Baden-Powell, who as Inspector of Cavalry was listed as a Vice-Patron of the Tournament in 1907.

Plymouth Hoe, including Sir Francis Drake. The second scene featured the speech at Tilbury by Queen Elizabeth I, addressing her troops in anticipation of a possible landing from the Spanish Armada.

In 1913 the Pageant focussed on the restoration of King Charles II. It was arranged by Lt. Col. Sir Mark Sykes, MP and Mr Edmund Sandars. The pageant received rave reviews in the newspapers, commenting on the scale and detail of the display, suggesting that it was the best to date. The Green Howards also gave a historic display of old-time weapons and grenade exercise.

The Officers' Riding and Jumping Competition had begun in 1891, it was open to officers riding their own horses as well as those on Government owned ones, the name was changed in 1908 to the Officers' Horse Show Jumping Competition. In 1913, King George V presented a challenge cup, which became known as the King's Cup Competition, in later years this was opened to all ranks.

The 1914 Tournament included the Historical Spectacle, 'The Romans in Britain' once again arranged by Sykes and Sanders. The programme notes said that the display was intended to "describe the coming and going of the Roman Legionaries, the first regular and disciplined soldiers seen in these islands." Well-known music teacher and composer Sir Charles Stanford specially composed the incidental music.

Other displays in 1914 included the Musical Double Ride by 1st Life Guards (first week) and 5th (Princess Charlotte of Wales's) Dragoon Guards (second week) as well as a Rough Riding Display by the Riding Establishment, Royal Artillery. The Musical Drive was given by F Battery, Royal Horse Artillery. The Royal Navy Inter-Port Field Gun Competition took place during the afternoon performances, a separate (non-competitive) display of Field Gun Drill was given at each evening performance.

The Band of the Duke of York's School were listed as playing the Overture at each performance. Boys from the Queen Victoria School, Dunblane gave a display of Highland Dancing and the Boys of the Cadet Corps "H.M.S. Excellent" danced the "Sailors' Hornpipe".

Now in its 35th Year the Tournament was once again thriving. The experiment of moving to Olympia had paid off, the arena was regularly filled with hundreds of performers in the pageants and with the addition of the Field Gun Competition along with traditional favourites such as the Musical Ride and Musical Drive the audience were attending in good numbers. The records show a charitable donation of £7,500 in 1914. However, 1914 was to be the last Tournament for some years. The show closed on 30 May, the assassination of Archduke Franz Ferdinand just a few weeks later began a series of events which plunged Europe into conflict by the end of July.

18 - The Royal Naval & Military Tournament Programme 1914

SIX – A NEW BEGINNING

The impact of the Great War was unprecedented, its influence was wide ranging, affecting not just the military population but society in general. At the start of the conflict, the British Force numbered, 700,000 trained soldiers (250,000 Regulars, 250,000 Territorials, and 200,000 Reservists). Enthusiastic volunteers from across the country began joining up during the summer of 1914. However, by 1916 conscription was introduced in order to meet the growing demands of the conflict. By the end of the war in 1918, the force had grown to more than 4 million soldiers. This swelling of numbers along with the tragic loss of 880,000 British Forces during the conflict, meant that the public were now closer to their Army than they ever had been.

Technology also moved forward at pace between 1914 and 1918. The war saw the first tank battles and the first aircraft carrier, it also saw the first aerial dogfights in Europe. Early wireless communication began, along with the first use of filmed propaganda. On the frontline, steel helmets were introduced, along with gas masks following the first chemical attacks. The Royal Air Force (RAF) was formed on 1 April 1918 following the amalgamation of the Royal Flying Corps (RFC) and the Royal Naval Air Service (RNAS).

After the Armistice in November 1918, plans were put in place and the Tournament returned with a new name the following year. The Royal Naval, Military, and AirForce Tournament opened at Olympia on 26 June 1919. The RAF provided two displays for their first appearance at the show. During the Afternoon Performances, a plane arrived in the arena on a flatbed vehicle and was unloaded and prepared for a reconnaissance flight, however immediately as it was ready for flight, an orderly arrived with "fresh instructions that the machine is to proceed at once by road to another aerodrome." The RAF ground crew then reloaded the plane onto its flatbed, leaving the arena to the applause of the enthusiastic audience.

During the Evening performances, with the arena in darkness, a "hostile machine" was "located crashed near a French Village." Workshop and transport vehicles entered the arena to recover the plane along with an ambulance and crew, who attended to the injured enemy pilot. The audience at Olympia were witnessing cutting edge technology, it was only 16 years since the Wright Brothers had made their first powered flight. During the Great War, aviation became a key asset to the battlefield. A small part of these tactics was now on show in the arena at Olympia for the appreciative audience. Although it was never possible to 'fly' a plane at the Tournament, various aircraft made their appearances over the years in the arena and in the static displays outside the arena which gave the audience the opportunity to see the aeroplanes (and other vehicles) at close hand.

In place of a pageant in 1919 a combined display was reintroduced, the army demonstrated "The Attack". With the enemy holding two lines of trenches in the arena which came under (simulated) artillery bombardment, one line at a time. British tanks led the assault, followed by infantry fighting their way forward through wire and into the enemy trenches. The Royal Engineers joined the assault, constructing a bridge over the trenches before the Royal Artillery brought forward their guns to continue the barrage. The audience were witnessing a depiction of the recent war at first hand. Although it was a stylised, theatrical, small-scale reenactment of the battle it would have been an impressive display.

For the first time, the Musical Ride was provided by an overseas army in 1919. The French Cavalry Musical Ride was led by three officers from the Saumur Cavalry School along with Non-Commissioned Officers from various French Regiments (Cuirassiers, Dragoons, Chasseurs, and Hussars) who had served with distinction during the War. The display was supported by a band of 25 trumpeters on horseback.

The first post Great War Tournament also included a demonstration of "Physical Training" as carried out "in the Field by Armies in France", a Machine Gun Display, and "Wheel Changing, and Driving Competition (For Women Motor Drivers)".

Another display which made its first appearance at the Tournament in 1919 was a demonstration of "Platoon Drill and the Handling of Arms" by "King's Squad" Royal Marines Light Infantry (R.M.L.I.). King George V had given permission for the title to be given to the senior recruit squad, during a visit to the Royal Marine Depot in 1918. This was the first of many displays by the King's Squad at the Tournament up to the 1990s.

The new name for the show only lasted for one year, the title was shortened to "The Royal Tournament" in 1920 and would remain the same until 1999.

There was a subtle change to the way that the printed programme listed the displays in 1920. The programme had always listed the items that would appear at each performance, matinee or evening for each of the days of the Tournament run, as the content would differ from day to day, performance to performance. For example:

Thursday Afternoon 26th June 1919

2.30 pm Royal Naval and Marine Inter-Port Field Gun Competition
2.50 pm Tug-of-War Metropolitan Police v Brighton Police
3.00 pm Demonstration of Physical Training
... and so on ...

From 1920 the events were still listed separately for each performance but were now numbered (rather than timed). An explanatory note in the 1923 programme stated, "Events will not necessarily be performed in the order shown, but the number of the event will be displayed at either end of the Arena." This convention lasted up until the 1970s. The Steward of the Arena (later the Officer in Charge of the Arena and Displays) would choose the order of the events for each performance, in the style of the Music Hall, this could change mid-show if needed. The performers backstage would listen out to be called forward to enter the arena for their event as the Steward required.

The RAF returned in 1920 with a physical training display by students from the RAF School of Technical Training, Halton. The King's Squad R.M.L.I. also returned with another display of Drill and Handling of Arms. The Royal Army Service Corps Display showed the various forms of transport used in different theatres of war, including Pack Ponies, Mules, Yak, and Zebu as well as Dog Sleigh Teams and Horse Drawn Wagons and the more modern 'Mechanical Transport'.

The Musical Ride was performed by 17th (Duke of Cambridge's Own) Lancers. 36 NCO's and Men performed the ride in 1920, 9 of which had served with the Regiment during the Great War. Four of the horses on display had also served during the war, they were denoted by the ribbon of the 1914 Star on their browbands. The programme notes also encouraged the audience to visit the stables following the afternoon performance, another tradition which continued for many years at the Tournament.

The Grand Pageant of that year was entitled "I Remember." The forward reads "A peaceful corner of a London park attracts the veterans of our Services. Time may dim the memory of the pensioners, but, arising from incidents of the Great War, recollections come streaming back and recall the past uniforms and drill." The object of the Pageant was to "show the past and pre-war full dress of the Royal Navy and Army in contrast to the working kit of the Great War."

The display included detachments from the Royal Navy, Royal Marines, and various Regiments of the Army dressed in period uniforms from 1805, 1815, and 1855 and concluded with music from the drummers of the 1st Bn Grenadier Guards along with a drill demonstration, loading and firing muskets, and forming square.

Pageants were popular through most of the twenties, the Royal Navy took the lead in 1921 with Neptune's Soldiers, telling the story of the sea soldiers from the time of the Roman occupation to the Royal Marines of the 1920s. Neptune himself, trident in hand, made an appearance in a chariot draw by three prancing white horses to introduce the pageant. The cavalcade of historic sea soldiers included Ancient Britons carry coracles, Viking marauders, Tudor Soldiers, and Marines in the dress of the Duke of York and Albany's Maritime Regiment from 1664. Marines from 1704 (Capture of Gibraltar) and from Nelson's fleet at Trafalgar were joined by their more recent counterparts who gave a display of drill.

The Grand Pageant of 1923, Scotland in Arms was produced by Captain A. Stirling, Argyll and Sutherland Highlanders. The final tableau included representatives from the Scottish Regiments in various period dress including Highlanders and Lowland Soldiers from the 16th and 17th century, Soldiers in the uniforms from Corunna, Waterloo, Balaclava, and the Great War. The musical accompaniment provided by Massed Pipes & Drums, playing traditional tunes: Highland Laddie, Scots wha' hae, and Black Bear.

The Territorial Force changed its name to the Territorial Army (TA) in 1921. Two Companies from the TA provided a reenactment at the Royal Tournament in 1923, however, as 'part time' soldiers the display took place on "Evenings Only, Twice Saturdays" according to the printed programme. The 23rd London Armoured Car Co. (Sharpshooters), assisted by 22nd Armoured Car Co. (Westminster Dragoons) recreated an incident from Western Egypt during 1916 when an armoured car column rescued Sailors from H.M.S. Tara who had been held captive since the previous November.

Also, at the evening performances in 1923, the 1st Air Defence Brigade (Royal Artillery & Royal Engineers) gave a display titled 'A Zeppelin Raid by Night'. With the arena in darkness, a flare was launched to signify an approaching Zeppelin, searchlights mounted on vehicles were then trained on the hostile (model) aircraft, moving from the west end of the arena. It was engaged by anti-aircraft guns, before disappearing behind a cloud. The Zeppelin was hit while behind the cloud and then fell to the floor in flames. Raids by German Zeppelins during WWI had brought the battlefront to the British mainland for the first time, displays such as this would have helped reinforce the public confidence of British air defences.

Celebrating the Royal Navy past and present, the pageant of 1924 was entitled 'Hearts of Oak', covering the period from Sir Francis Drake to the 1920s. The 1924 Tournament also included the first combined physical training display with 80 men drawn from the Royal Navy, Royal Marines, Army, and Royal Air Force. The display included a series of massed exercises and maze marching. Maze marching displays involved large numbers of athletes forming elaborate patterns in the arena often set to music. Marching in close order, the display teams would appear to act in unison, forming pin-wheels, lines and boxes. In the finale of this combined display the various groups constructing human pyramids.

The Royal Artillery staged their own pageant in 1925 entitled 'Ubique, part of the motto of the Royal Artillery, which means "everywhere". The pageant opened with a fanfare played by the mounted trumpeters of the Royal Artillery Depot. It included the birth of the Royal Regiment of Artillery in 1716, The Battle of Minden (1759), The Siege of Gibraltar (1779-83), the first Royal Horse Artillery (1793), and the Rocket Troop of the RHA (1813). The pageant continued with a Musical Drive by "O" Battery, RHA representing the Peninsular War and Waterloo Period. The pageant concluded with guns from the Great War and a tableau including the guns from across the history of the Royal Artillery.

The combined display was revived in 1926 in place of a pageant, bringing together elements of the Royal Artillery, Royal Engineers, and infantry in a 'Frontier Fight'. The Royal Navy and Royal Marines played the part of enemy tribesmen at each performance.

In 1927 the Great Pageant was simply called 'Scotland'. It included a reenactment of the Battle of Killiecrankie (first Jacobite Rising) followed by a display of Highland Dancing. The third part of the pageant was titled "Unity", it depicted the formation of the Scottish Regiments to fight for the United Kingdom. Massed Pipes & Drums from the Scottish regiments provided the musical accompaniment for the pageant.

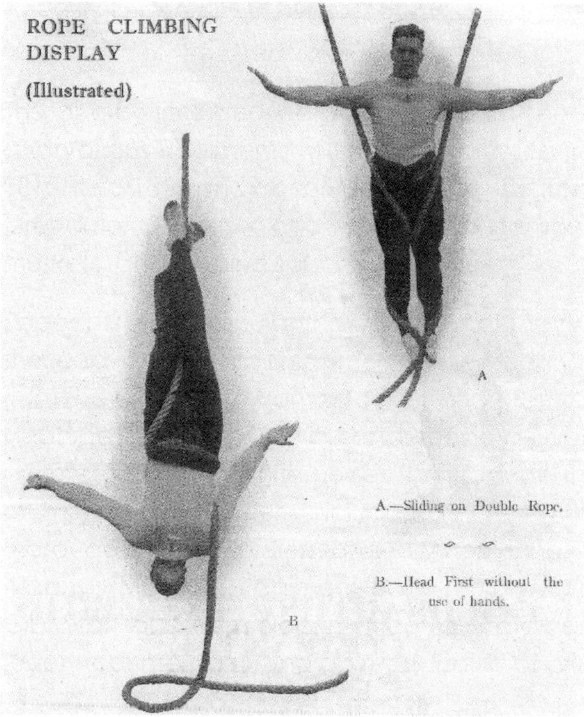

19 - Rope Climbing Display (1927 Programme)

The Royal Navy gave a display of Rope Climbing at the 1927 Tournament. 60 men from the Royal Navy and Royal Marines took part in the display, climbing 66 ropes hung at 3 ft intervals from the roof of Olympia. The display included ascending (using both hands and feet), various typed of descending; feet first (hand under hand), head first (hand under hand), feet first (without using the feet), feet first (sliding on double rope), and head first without the use of the hands (swallow dive). The display also included "Side Travelling" from rope-to-rope "in time to music."

Boys from the Duke of York's School first took part in the Tournament in 1884, providing a guard of honour and playing the National Anthem during the arrival of the Duke of Cambridge. In 1928, the school provided a Toy Soldier Display. A picture book containing photos was produced for this display (as was done for many of the pageants during this period) it included notes on the origins of the display. It refers to a young girl who asked her parents for a set of miniature soldiers, she paraded them "according to her own idea," her older brother (a soldier himself) "showed her how her soldiers should parade". The pupils of the Duke of York's School played the part of the little girl's toy soldiers in the different formations, at the end of the display they all fall flat as the she "grew tired and weary of them" swooping her arm across the ranks! The display was repeated by the school in 1935 and 1937.

From 1928, pageants became Historic Displays (or Episodes). With a different regiment taking the lead each year, highlighting elements of their regimental history. In the first year, the 1st Bn Royal Scots Fusiliers took the lead. A modern-day guard of honour accompanied by their band, pipes, and drums entered the arena and presented arms to the Royal Box. The guard then retired to the four corners of the arena to settle down for the night. While 'sleeping', they dream of their history, predecessors at the Battle of Inkerman and squads dressed in period uniform going back to their formation in 1678 through their time in Nova Scotia, at the Battle of Waterloo, and the Great War. A spectacular and colourful history lesson for the Olympia audience.

In their Historic Display in 1929, the 1st Bn. Middlesex Regiment (formerly 57th Regiment of Foot) reenacted an episode from the Battle of Albuera in 1811 during the Peninsular War when Colonel William Inglis was wounded and refused to be carried from the battlefield. He was heard to calmly repeat the phrase "Die hard 57th, die hard!", earning the regimental nickname of the "Die-Hards".

Following the success of the Rope Climbing Display in 1927, the Royal Navy returned in 1929 with a "Rope Climbing & Window Ladder Display". 80 men from the Royal Navy and Royal Marines ascended ropes and performed "various exercises on the Gymnasium Window Ladders". Five sets of Window Ladders with ropes attached were suspended from the barrel-vaulted roof of Olympia.

In 1930, the 2nd Bn, The Royal Fusiliers depicted the formation of the Fusiliers at the Tower of London in 1685. They also highlighted their historic links to the Navy, having previously served as marine troops, and that their first Colonel (George Lord Dartmouth) was also Admiral of the Fleet. In their Historic display the following year (1931), the 2nd Bn, The Gloucestershire Regiment once again used the memories of old soldiers to illustrate their regimental history. Chelsea Pensioners from the forbearer regiments, 28th (North Gloucestershire) and 61st (South Gloucestershire) met outside "Ye Sphynx Tavern" to "gossip over old times in the Regiment" while their historic memories from South Africa, Delhi, and Sebastopol were reenacted in the arena.

Another 'first' for the Royal Tournament came in 1931 with a Motorcycle Display by Despatch Riders of the Training Battalion, Royal Corps of Signals. The programme notes explain that motorcycles were first introduced to the Army in 1914, when volunteers, riding their own motorcycles, joined the Signal Service, Royal Engineers. Transferring to the Royal Corps of Signals on its formation in 1920, 'Despatch Rider' became one of the Signal Trades. New Despatch Riders underwent a twenty week course at Catterick, learning to ride and navigate over "any kind of country, in all weathers."

This first display was performed by six solo riders to give an "idea of the riding capabilities of the trained Despatch Rider" and the "controllability of the modern motorcycle", it was also "enlivened by certain humorous acrobatics with a motorcycle and sidecar". Motorcycles for the display were supplied by the Triumph Motorcycle Company, a tradition still in place for the final motorcycle display by the White Helmets at the 1999 Tournament.

The motorcycle displays proved to be popular with the audience, the Royal Signals returned in 1932 with a display by 8 solo riders. In 1933, as mechanisation of the corps was well underway, they provided a combined display with riders on horseback and on motorcycles.

The 1st Bn. The Prince of Wales's Volunteers delved further into history in 1932 as they presented "The First Prince of Wales, The Legend of Edward of Caernarvon". The full Band and Drums, under the direction of Bandmaster Mr P. Ryan, played traditional Welsh music including 'Men of Harlech' and 'Land of My Fathers'. The huge cast included 24 Caernarvon Castle Guards, 76 Men-At-Arms, 67 Welch Tribesmen, 29 Cross-Bowmen, 31 Long-Bowmen, and another 30 or so central characters which included Edward I, Queen Eleanor, Barons, Knights, Welch Chieftains, and Trumpeters. In addition, 8 Ladies-in-Waiting were "kindly arranged by The Royal Academy of Dramatic Art".

1933 was acknowledged as the 50th Tournament and was marked as a Jubilee, the programme notes included a "Short History of the Royal Tournament", referencing the competitions by the volunteers on Wimbledon Common in the 1870s, through the Islington days, and onto Olympia. It also noted the considerable amount of money raised for service charities (averaging £24,000 per year from 1919 to 1933, equivalent to £1 Million in 2025)[13].

Brigadier-General Sir Wallis King stepped down from the role of Hon. Secretary and Manager in 1934, a role that he took on in 1911 although he had been a part of the Tournament since becoming Assistant Hon. Treasurer in 1897. He retained Chairmanship of the General Purposes Sub-Committee and was still listed in the programme under the title of 'Administration' until 1939. The role of Secretary passed to his son Captain (later Major) C.W.C. King, Royal Army Service Corps. He had been officially

[13] Source: Bank of England Inflation calculator website

associated with the Tournament since 1923 when he took on the role of Marshalling Officer but had been closely involved for many years previously supporting his father before joining the Army himself. He continued in the role of Secretary for 20 years, handing over to Lieutenant Colonel A.V. Webb after the 1954 Royal Tournament. Between father and son, the family had been involved in the event for a period of 57 years.

The Historic Display of 1934 was presented by 2nd Battalion, The Black Watch (Royal Highlanders) telling the story of the regiment from the mid-eighteenth century in Flanders, Waterloo, Egypt, The Great War, and on to the 1930s.

The 1935 Tournament was headed by "The Spirit of Co-Operation – A Combined Display by the Three Services". The scenes were set in Portsmouth and included performers from H.M.S. Excellent, Queen's Royal Regiment, Royal Air Force, and "Ladies from the Royal Academy of Dramatic Art". The display included: Arrival of King Charles II in Portsmouth to meet his future wife in 1662, followed by scenes entitled "The Army Serves with the Navy Afloat" (1794), "The Navy Serves with the Army Ashore" (1902), and "Spirit of Co-Operation (1935).

Another patriotic display in 1936, saw the 2nd Battalion, The Royal Norfolk Regiment reenact the Historic Episode "Armada Days in Norfolk". The display told the story of the visit to Norfolk by Queen Elizabeth's General, Sir Thomas Leighton during the spring of 1588 to inspect the trained soldiers of the County. In the display, members of the Battalion in period dress, armed with Pikes and Muskets lined the route for the arrival of the General. The Band and Drums (dressed in present day uniforms) entered the arena to the quick march, 'The Royal Standard.' The General was met by the Mayor of Norwich and went on to read a message from Queen Elizabeth. At the end of the display, the massed cast marched off to the Slow March 'Merrie England' and the Regimental March 'Rule Britannia.'

There was a notable omission at the 1936 Tournament, there was no Field Gun Competition. The headline in the Portsmouth Evening News on 7 May said, "Olympia Without Field Guns". The report went on to say that the "Navy and Marines are well represented in the Tournament by their latest recruits, while their more seasoned comrades are abroad." They mention the "drafting demands of the international situation, the Service has been unable to spare the men or the time to send guns' crews to Olympia." This is thought to be related to the Abyssinian Crisis, a conflict between Italy and Ethiopia (then known as Abyssinia). The Competition was once again part of the Tournament programme in 1937.

The Territorial Army played an increasing part in the Tournaments of the 1930s. In 1935, the Massed Drums and Fifes of 167th Infantry Brigade (Territorial Army) provided a display. The following year (1936) an Air Defence Display was given by 26th (London) Anti-Aircraft Group and 1st Anti-Aircraft Divisional Signals, both from the TA. The Honourable Artillery Company provided a Historical Display in 1937, marking their 400th year of its incorporation by Royal Charter of King Henry VIII. In the same year, the motorcycle display was given by members of the City of London Signals (TA).

As the storm clouds began to gather over Europe, the London Territorials provided two displays: Modern Infantry Fight (1938) and Modern Display (1939). The country wasn't on a war footing yet, but it was clear that the part-time soldiers of the TA would play an important role in any future conflict and the Tournament gave the public an opportunity to see the competence of these reservists from the comfort of their seats at Olympia.

Although there were no pageants in the 1938 or 1939 Tournaments, the tradition of massed band performances was being established. The Massed Pipe Bands of the Scottish Regiments performed in 1938 with highland dancing by soldiers from The Scots Guards, Cameronians (Scottish Rifles), Seaforth Highlanders, and Queen's Own Cameron Highlanders. The Massed Bands of the Royal Marines[14] provided musical support to the Royal Marines Drill Display in 1939.

The 1939 programme included a Physical Training Display by students from the Army School of Physical Training as well as a display of club swinging and maze movements by the Royal Air Force, Uxbridge. The Musical Ride was provided by The Life Guards and The Musical Drive by "K" Battery, Royal Horse Artillery. In addition to the Modern Display by the London Territorials each evening, the 2nd Battalion Grenadier Guards gave a display of some 'Modern Infantry Weapons'. The RAF gave a Technical Display, showing a Balloon Barrage being unloaded, inflated, flown, hauled down, deflated, repacked, and moved off to another location. The

[14] The first recorded Massed Bands of HM Royal Marines, 64 musicians from Chatham, Portsmouth, and Plymouth.

second half of the display showed how aircrew had been trained in the use of parachutes, described as the "life-belt of the air".

The Boys of the Duke of York's Royal Military School returned to the Tournament in 1939, this time, the Toy Soldiers took part in a Mimic Battle. Dressed in white trousers, with red and blue tunics, and tall black hats, the carried wooden rifles and marched with straight legs, as if they were made of tin. They formed up in front of the Royal Box where they presented arms before performing a short Drill Display. A large-scale model fort and two guns were placed at one end of the arena, the red soldiers moved to defend the fort and the blue setup to attack it. The blue soldiers were the victors at each performance. A bugle was sounded at the end of the display and all the casualties and survivors formed up in front of the Royal Box once more, before marching off, led by the school band.

20 - Royal Tournament Programme 1939

The list of Executive Staff in the 1939 programme includes Hon. Advisor to Displays, Henry Sherek. This is the only record of his involvement with the Royal Tournament. Sherek had served in the Rifle Brigade during WWI, he made his name later as a theatre producer, he was responsible for staging over 100 plays in London, Paris, and New York, including works by T.S. Eliot. He returned to the Army during WWII, promoted to Major before being invalided out in 1944. It's not clear if his involvement in 1939 was meant to be a 'one-off' or if he had been engaged to advise on a long-term basis.

The 1939 Royal Tournament closed on 3 June. Three months later, following the invasion of Poland, Great Britain and France declared war on Germany. The Tournament was once again paused, as Europe entered the second major conflict of the twentieth century.

SEVEN – POST-WAR BOOM

It is something of an understatement to say that the Second World War had another huge impact on the British population. Conscription meant that most families could count a serviceman or servicewoman amongst their number. There was a feeling that everyone had 'done their bit' for the war effort, in essential services, on farms, in factories, as Air Raid Precaution (ARP) Warden's, in the Home Guard, on the Homefront, and overseas. Bombing raids by the German Luftwaffe had also brought the British Public closer to the conflict than most people could have imagined in the years leading up to the war.

By the time the first post-war Tournament was staged in June 1947, the country was starting to rebuild and the demobilisation of millions of men and women back into 'civvy street' was well underway. Major C.W.C. King and his assistant Captain V.C. Soggee had been released from their war service in time to make arrangements for the 1947 Tournament at Olympia.

21 - Royal Tournament Programme Cover 1947

Familiar favourites such as the Royal Naval Field Gun Competition returned, along with a drill display by the King's Squad, RM, and a motorcycle display by the Royal Signals. There were also physical training displays by all three services, music from the massed pipe bands, and a trick riding display by the Royal Army Veterinary Corps. However, there was no Musical Drive in 1947 although the cover image for the programme that year was a Gilbert Holiday painting of a pre-war Musical Drive.

In another first, the newly formed Royal Marine Commandos gave a display entitled "A raid against an enemy-held coastline." Formed in June 1940, following a request from Winston Churchill for a special force to conduct raids on German-occupied Europe, this was the first of many appearances at the

Royal Tournament for the Commandos. The post-war audience numbers were strong, and the committee donated £27,000 to armed forces charities in 1947.

The Field Gun Crews from Portsmouth, Devonport, and Chatham were joined by a fourth crew, Naval Air Command (later known as Fleet Air Arm) in 1947. At this point the record was held by Devonport Stokers, a time of 3 min. 48 secs, set in 1938. Naval Air Command reduced this to 3 min. 38 3/5 secs in 1949.

From 1896 until 1939 (with the exception of the First World War), the Musical Drive had been performed at the Tournament by the resident Royal Horse Artillery Battery at St John's Wood Barracks, see Appendix C. Prior to mechanization, Horse Artillery had been a key tactical asset on the battlefield, the RHA Batteries rotated their home barracks every two to three years.

Following the Second World War in 1946 a Mounted Ceremonial Battery of Artillery was formed by Royal Decree to fire salutes on state occasions, dressed in the traditional style. They were initially known as The Riding Troop. However, on his first inspection of the Troop at St John's Wood in November 1947 King George VI crossed out the name 'Riding' and replacing it with the word 'King's' in the visitors book. The official title of The King's Troop Royal Horse Artillery was adopted and from 1948 onwards, they provided the spectacular Musical Drive[15] each year at the Royal Tournament.

The 1948 show included a Physical Training Display by the "Women's Auxiliary Services" another first for the Tournament and an indication of how Women had started to become more integrated into the Armed Forces. The first post-war Musical Ride was given by the Household Cavalry,

[15] The Tournament Drive, as it was known is still practiced each year by the King's Troop as a means of training new horses and riders. In 2012, the troop relocated from St John's Wood to Woolwich.

a recreation of the Ceremony of the Keys was given by 2nd Battalion Scots Guards, and Massed Bands of the Royal Navy School of Music also performed.

Another audience favourite made its debut at the 1949, "The Royal Air Force Police Dogs on Parade presented by the Royal Air Force Provost Branch". The display included 70 Alsatian dogs and their handlers. Each dog had their own kennel, painted in RAF Colours with a plaque showing their name, the dogs were "on view" to the public between performances. There was a tradition for many years at the Tournament, that the stables were open to the public between performances as well, this was stopped in the 1980s as security around the Tournament was tightened.

The Tournament audience was again given a unique insight into new military tactics in 1949 when the RAF Transport Command gave a display of parachute training. The first parachute training school at Ringway, Manchester had only opened eight years earlier, in November 1941. In the display, the techniques of parachute training were demonstrated by RAF Physical Training Instructors and other personnel using standard training equipment. The display team included an RAF Airwoman and an RAF Nursing Sister. The parachutists were raised 100 ft to the ceiling of Olympia before making a controlled decent back to the arena floor – something that had not been seen in public before.

The Royal Engineers held a Bridge Building Competition in 1949, demonstrating the rapid bridge building that had taken place during recent operations in Europe. There were four Teams in the competition with two competing at each performance, on the signal to start they began building their bridge, once completed a vehicle was driven over it to "ensure that it had been correctly constructed." The winning team was awarded 2 points in the competition. The team with the most points across the whole Tournament were awarded the trophy.

With the exception of the World Wars, the Tournament had been a regular feature of the London 'Summer Season' since its inception in 1880. In 1950, now in its sixtieth edition, the Tournament made the short move (approx. 1 mile) from Olympia along Warwick Road to Earls Court Exhibition Centre.

* * *

The first event staged on the site of the later Earls Court Exhibition Centre, was the 1887 American Exhibition. The organiser, John Robinson Whitley, had delayed the event by a year following protests from the then Prince of Wales, as the event was originally planned to run at the same time as a British Colonial and Indian Exhibition stage nearby at South Kensington. During the twelve-month delay, Whitley met Colonel William Frederic Cody (Buffalo Bill) during a visit to Washington. Whitley secured the rights to bring Cody's Wild West Show to London as part of the American Exhibition, the show occupied the triangular parcel of land which would become home to the Earls Court Exhibition Centre fifty years later.

From this first event, the site evolved into glorious showgrounds, holding numerous temporary national exhibitions over the following years. Additions to the showground in 1896 included the 6,000 capacity Empress Theatre and a 300 ft high 'Gigantic Wheel' which could carry 1,200 passengers. The showground closed to the public in 1914 and was used as a reception and processing centre for refugees during the Great War.

The site was given a new lease of life in the 1930s. A venue was required to stage the British Industries Fair (First staged at the Royal Agricultural Hall in 1915). A new company, Earls Court Ltd, was formed to develop the site as a versatile new modern venue with 42,000 m^2 of exhibition space along with a 23,000-capacity auditorium, and a 30m x 60m (4m deep) swimming pool. The Exhibition Centre was connected to Earls Court Station via a tunnel under Warwick Road.

The building works were delayed due to strikes and the shortage of steel as the country was now rearming, which took priority over construction projects. The Chocolate and Confectionary Exhibition was the first show to open at the new venue on 1 September 1937, the Motor Show and Commercial Vehicle Show soon followed. The Ideal Home Exhibition was planned to relocate from Olympia in 1937 but due to the delays it didn't make the move until 1939.

The venue was temporarily closed later that year, as Britain entered the Second World War, Earls Court Exhibition Centre was requisitioned by the War Office for the manufacture of the barrage balloons and was undamaged during the German bombing campaign. Olympia suffered light bomb damage on six occasions during the war, the building had also been requisitioned. It was used initially as a base for the Free French Army, then as a Transport Depot, later a Clothing Store, and finally as a demobilisation centre before the Tournament Returned in June 1947.

* * *

The 1950 programme notes say that the Tournament had relocated due to its "ever-increasing popularity" stating that "no other building in London can now accommodate the numbers who wish to see it". This was a boom period for the show, the crowds flocked to support their Armed Forces, there was a sense of pride and patriotism with those who had lived through the recent conflict.

22 - Royal Marine Commandos assaulted their Last Cliff at the 1999 Royal Tournament

The Royal Marine Commandos once again conducted "A raid against an enemy-held coastline", the display was enhanced from that seen at Olympia by the sheer scale of the venue. Earls Court was designed with seating on three sides, enabling a huge backcloth to be constructed on the fourth side at one end of the arena. In 1950 (as in many years following) the backcloth included a cliff face, which the Commandos expertly climbed before 'neutralising' their objective which in this year a bridge painted high up in the backcloth scenery. The 'Extraction' involved Marines returning to the arena floor by fast roping or using the "Death Slide," much to the delight of the children in the audience.

In addition, Earls Court offered a complete 'blackout' of the arena, unlike the glazed roofs of Olympia and the Royal Agricultural Hall, allowing 'night-time raids' to be conducted in the arena during the matinee performances as well as in the evenings!

The organisers quickly adapted the show for the new venue. The naming convention for the building used the roads around Earls Court as reference points; the Warwick Road Entrance, West Brompton Entrance, and the (lesser used, often forgotten) Philbeach Entrance for example. This followed into the arena. The end opposite the backcloth became known as the Warwick Road End (with arena entrances in each corner). The West Brompton side of the arena became home to the Royal Box and was usually referred to as the 'Royal Box Side' during the performance. The opposite side was known as the Philbeach side (or non-Royal Box Side[16]).

The Royal Box had been located on the balcony level at Olympia. A section of the balustrade could be removed on either side of the Royal Box to allow the VIP to make their way through the seating area in front (The Royal Enclosure) to inspect the Guard of Honour, present Prizes etc. The Royal Box Guests would arrive by car at the Hammersmith Road entrance, make their way on the Red Carpet through the National Hall and take the lift to the balcony level before accessing the Royal Box in the adjacent Grand Hall.

The Royal Box at Earls Court was built at the rear of the stalls on the West Brompton Side. VIP guests would access the rear of the Royal Box and ground level via a Red Carpet from the VIP entrance (on the side of the building between the Warwick and West Brompton Road entrances). A special (temporary) lift was bought by Earls Court to enable VIP Guests to avoid the 35-step staircase to the seating area above. It was installed each year of the Tournament up until the Last Run in 1999.

Another feature of the new venue was the high ceiling above the arena, this enabled the RAF to conduct a more convincing display of parachute training. At Olympia, the parachutists were hoisted into position (in full view of the audience) before descending on cue to the arena floor. At Earls Court, the removal of a few ceiling tiles meant that the parachutists could access their stepping off point out of view of the audience before making their dramatic descent to the arena floor – a tactic which would be used many times over the next 50 years. The number of performances was increased from 30 to 32 in 1950. The show opened on Wednesday 7 June, with two performances each day (except Sundays) until Saturday 24 June.

The Gordon Boys' School from Woking in Surrey provided a display in 1950. In a variation to the Toy Soldier Displays, the school provided the "Gordon Cavalry". 64 boys took part, dressed as knights on horseback with false legs

[16] The Field Gun Crews referred to the side of the arena for their run as either Royal Side or Non-Royal Side.

hanging from their waists, they trotted and cantered around the arena in an unusual take on the Musical Ride.

The 1950 programme also listed 16 bands from the Sea Cadet Corps, Army Cadet Force, and Air Training Corps. The bands performed for twenty-five minutes each evening from 19:00 hrs before the main performance started, a tradition which continued for many years. The Honourable Artillery Company provided a Pike and Musket Display at each evening performance. The programme also noted that Skill-At-Arms (Dismounted) Competitions would take place in the "Convention Banquet Hall, on the second Mezzanine Floor", the competitions were relocated to the exhibition floor near the West Brompton Entrance the following year, which was clearly easier to find for the audience.

The Window Ladder and Rope Climbing Display was performed for the first time at Earls Court in 1951. Volunteers from all branches of the Royal Navy and Royal Marines were trained by the Royal Naval School of Physical Training for the display, which was conducted at a height of 50 ft above the arena.

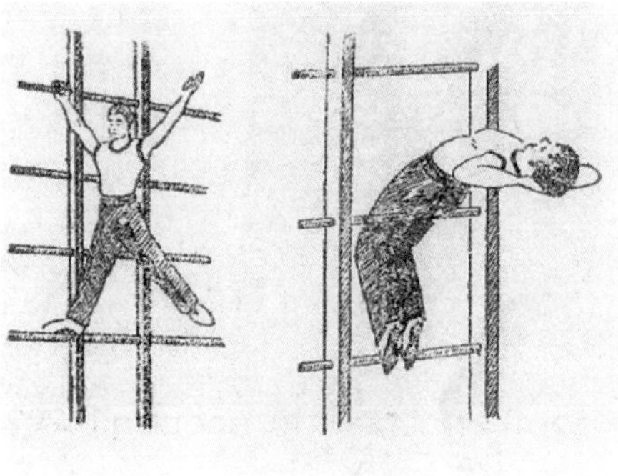

23 - Diagrams of the Window Ladder Display (1953 Programme)

The Royal Military School of Music at Kneller Hall, Twickenham, provided the musicians for the 1951 Tournament. The band and fanfare trumpeters were made up of 40 Student Bandmasters and 220 Pupils under training at Kneller Hall, representing 75 different Corps and Regiments. The Director of Music was Major Meredith Roberts, the musical programme included traditional music such as 'The Minstrel Boy', 'Men of Harlech', and 'Here's a Health unto His Majesty'.

His Majesty King George VI attended the opening performance on the afternoon of 6 June 1951. He was greeted by Guards of Honour from the Royal Navy, Brigade of Guards, and the Royal Air Force. Unknown at the time, this was to be his last visit to the Royal Tournament. Following his death on 6 February 1952, the nation entered a new Elizabethan era.

The young Princesses Elizabeth and Margaret had been regular visitors to the Royal Tournament, accompanying their parents to Olympia from the mid-1930s. The new Queen Elizabeth II attended the opening of the Tournament on 4 June 1952 for the first time as monarch, she went on to attend right up to the final year of the Royal Tournament in 1999.

The Royal Air Force Regiment was formed in 1942; to celebrate their 10th Anniversary, a Continuity Drill display was performed at the 1952 Tournament for the first time. The display was executed "as a continuous series of movements without words of command" intended to show that "men can be trained in the co-ordination of mind and body to develop perfect team-work and precision in movement." The programme notes also gave some interesting stats about the display team; the average age of the aircraftmen taking part was 19 and their average height was 6 feet. Their average length of service was 8 ½ months and 20% of the team were National Service Airmen. This popular display returned in 1954 and from 1960 onwards Continuity Drill Displays were given by the Queen's Colour Squadron[17], the RAF's dedicated ceremonial unit.

The Massed Bands from Kneller Hall returned in 1952, with a slightly smaller contingent of 40 Student Bandmasters and 185 Pupils. The RAF provided a display of "Illuminated Club Swinging", taking advantage of the darkness that could be created in the arena at Earls Court. The display was given by recruits (with less than 3 months service) from No. 7 School of Recruit Training. There was also a display of physical training from the more experienced P.T. Instructors from the Royal Navy, Royal Marines, Army and RAF. In this combined display, the instructors showed their agility with 'chair tricks' and mat exercises before progressing to vaulting over the high box horse.

The programme also included an advert for "The Story of the Royal Tournament" by Lt. Col. Binns which was published in this year by Gale & Polden Limited. Visitors were encouraged to pick up a copy from their stand, close to the main entrance. Gale & Polden was founded in Kent in 1868, moving to Aldershot in the 1893, the company had a long association with the Tournament publishing books, programmes, and souvenir postcards.

---

[17] On the demise of Her Late Majesty Queen Elizabeth II, the Squadron became the custodians of the King's Colour and was renamed the King's Colour Squadron on 27 October 2022. Reference: https://raf.mod.uk/

24 - A well-loved copy of The Story of the Royal Tournament by Lt. Co. Binns (belonging to the Author)

The Coronation of Her Majesty Queen Elizabeth II took place on Tuesday 2 June 1953. The Tournament was moved back by a week to open on 10 June, however the accommodation at Earls Court opened in late May to billet the troops from across the country and abroad who took part in the coronation procession.

Some of the Colonial and Dominion Troops stayed on in London and participated in the Royal Tournament as well. The Coronation Contingent of the Royal Canadian Mounted Police performed a Musical Ride. 32 NCO's and Constables, drawn from across the force took part in the display, riding black horses, dressed in their iconic red tunics and Stetson hats.

The finale of the 1953 show was entitled "The Crown". The Massed Bands of the Royal Marines, 4th/7th Royal Dragoon Guards, Royal Berkshire Regiment, as well as No. 1 and No. 2 Royal Air Force Regional Bands performed 'Crown Imperial' by William Walton, and 'Rose of England' by Ivor Novello. They were joined by detachments from Pakistan, Ceylon, Southern Rhodesia, and the Gurkhas who formed an illuminated crown in honour of the Queen's Coronation.

The Corps of Royal Electrical and Mechanical Engineers (R.E.M.E.) introduced another competition in 1953. The "Jeep Assembly Display" involved six regional R.E.M.E. Commands (four competing at each

25 - Royal Tournament Programme 1953

performance). Packing crates containing the components of a Jeep were delivered into the arena on trailers. The teams raced to unpack and assemble their Jeep, the winner being the first to drive the assembled vehicle across the finish line in front of the Royal Box. The fastest time in 1953 was 3 min. 0.5 secs, set by 4 Command Workshop R.E.M.E., the competition returned in 1954 and 1957.

Admiral Sir Rhoderick R. McGrigor, First Sea Lord, opened the Royal Tournament on 2 June 1954 (attended on 9 June). This ended the tradition of a Royal Visit on the opening day of the Tournament, going back to 1882 when Princess Mary Adelaide (Dutchess of Teck) opened the Grand Military Tournament at Islington.

Having previously demonstrated parachute training, the Royal Air Force, Maintenance Command, gave a display of "Modern Safety Equipment in Service Aircraft – The Ejection Seat" in 1954. In the first phase of the display, trainees demonstrated the ground training: jumping from low and high ramps, and from trailers towed across the arena. In the second phase, trainees sat in ejector seats which were fired up training towers to simulate ejection. In the final phase a Gloster Meteor Mk. 8 Aircraft was brought into the arena, the pilot was ejected and descended to safety by parachute!

There was a display of Massed Pipers and Drummers of the Scottish Regiments in 1954 under the direction of Lieutenant G.G. Allt of 1st Bn. King's Own Scottish Borderers. The Massed Bands of the Royal Marines also performed a Beating Retreat Ceremony. The Band of HM Royal Marines, Plymouth and the Band of the Royal Marines School of Music, Deal performed under the direction of Captain William Lang, RM. The musical programme included 'H.M. Jollies' (Alford), 'The Globe and Laurel' (arr. Dunn), and 'The Holy City' (Adams).

The Massed Bands of the Royal Air Force performed at the Royal Tournament for the first time in 1955 (appearing by permission of the Air Council). Under the direction of Conductor Wing Commander A. E. Sims, the Central Band of the RAF were joined by No. 1, No. 4, and No. 5 Regional Bands along with the Royal Air Force Regiment Band and the Central Band of the Women's Royal Air Force.

The musical programme for the display included: 'The Thunderer' (Sousa), 'National Emblem' (Bagley), and 'Finlandia' (Sibelius), it also included three pieces by Wg Cdr Sims; 'Elizabethan Echoes', 'March of the Royal Air Force Association', and an unnamed Fanfare.

Two overseas acts appeared at the 1955 Tournament, performing at alternate performances. The Pipes & Drums of the Pakistan Police was made up of representatives from the various Pipe Bands in the from across Pakistan, they performed with their mascot, a urial, a mountain sheep with 30-inch curved horns. The Pipes & Drums of the Arab Legion performed by permission of His Majesty King Hussain of Jordan.

The 1955 Tournament also included a Pageant of Infantry, showing the evolution of equipment and uniforms from the Battle of Crécy (1346) to the Peninsular War (1807–1814), and on to the 1950s. Making the point that, although the equipment and uniforms have evolved, the role of infantry; to close with and destroy the enemy, then to hold the ground, had not changed in 600 years.

Two more oversea acts took part in the 1956 Tournament, the Band of the Federation of Malaya Police and the Fort Henry Guard of Ontario, Canada. Fort Henry was a British Garrison in the Victorian Era; the Guard is made up of student volunteers who keep alive the traditions of the garrison to this day, conducting drill and firing displays and sunset ceremonies. They returned to perform at the Tournament in 1963. The Malaya Police Band was formed in 1932, by the mid-1950s the band was travelling 10,000 miles per year giving performances in towns and villages across Malaya.

The Royal Navy gave a display entitled "A Convoy Night Action" illustrating how convoys were defended in the Atlantic during the Second World War. The action moved from the British Maritime HQ to model ships in the arena. The 1956 Massed Bands were provided by the Light Infantry Brigade under the Direction of Bandmaster C.D. Jarrett. The musical programme included 'Jellalabad' (James). 'Waltzing Bugle Boy' (Martin), and 'Light Infantry' (Plater).

26 - Royal Tournament Programme 1957

The Massed Bands of the Royal Marines performed at the 1957 Tournament under the direction of Lieutenant Colonel F. Vivian Dunn. The music included 'Under the White Ensign', 'Commando Patrol', and 'Salute for Heroes' all composed by Lt. Col. Dunn. The music continued with the Massed Drums, Pipes, and Bugles of the North Irish Brigade, opening with a Bugle Fanfare, the display also included traditional tunes such as 'The Minstrel Boy' and 'St. Patrick's Day'.

The King's African Rifles performed at the 1957 Tournament; the theme of the display showed "the transformation of the East African tribesman into the trained King's African Rifles Askari (Soldier)". The soldiers performed tribal dances and a drill display, accompanied by their band.

The number of performances was reduced from 32 to 30 in 1957. There was no matinee on 5 June (the opening day) or on Monday 10 or 17 June. There were also no performances on Sunday, the performers and support staff had a day and a half off between the Saturday and Monday evening performances. This pattern continued until the 1990s.

In 1958, a National Service Airman by the name of Basil Reitz was chosen to provide the commentary[18] for the Royal Air Force presentation "Missile Defence". On four occasions that year, when the house commentator was unavailable, he stepped in to provide the commentary for the whole show. His National Service came to an end three days before the end of the show's run; however he stayed on for the final performances in what should have been his end-of-service (terminal) leave.

[18] Display teams often provided their own commentator who they would rehearse with prior to the Tournament, the house commentator would link between displays and commentate on those which didn't have their own.

Basil Reitz

Basil Reitz was born in Essex in 1932, he served as a National Service Airman with Headquarters 11 Group Fighter Command, completing his service in the summer of 1958.

Following his time in the RAF he returned to Essex, where he spent most of his life working in agriculture. From 1991 to 1993, he was a Director of the Royal Association of British Dairy Farmers – the organisation mentioned earlier which brought Raffety and Burnaby together in 1878.

His voice was familiar to generations of the Royal Tournament audiences as he commentated on the show for 41 years. He was awarded the MBE in the Queen's Birthday honours of 1984 for 'Services to the Royal Tournament'.

The Foreword of the 1958 programme was written by Field Marshal The Viscount Montgomery of Alamein and so began a new tradition of senior military officers showing their support for the Royal Tournament by providing a Foreword for the souvenir programme each year. The Foreword itself was not a new thing, the earliest programmes that I have seen while researching this book were from the 1890s and they all included an opening page outlining new items which would appear in the arena that year and highlighting the amount donated to charity in the previous year (or up to that date). Montgomery ended his note with "Whatever the future may hold, tradition, discipline and courage will always be required in our Services. Each year, since it was first performed in 1880, the Royal Tournament has shown the public how well these essentials are maintained and has provided much needed money for Service charities. Long may it continue."

The 1st Battalion, The Royal Sussex Regiment produced a pageant in 1959 called "The Inevitable Hour" marking the 200th anniversary of the Battle of Quebec. The Navy display was "A battle of Nuclear Submarines."

As the 1950s drew to a close, the Tournament had found its drumbeat following the disruption of the Second World War in the previous decade. Although the order of the displays could still be different from performance to performance, the Massed Bands would close the show. The Bands were rotating year on year; Army (Light Infantry) 1956, Royal Marines 1957, and Royal Air Force 1958.

There were also regular displays which would return to the Tournament every few years, including: Commando Raids and Window Ladder displays, RAF Police Dogs, Continuity Drill, Jeep Assembly, Musical Ride, as

27 - Royal Tournament Programme 1959

well as Physical Training and Gymnastics displays. Along with the annual favourites of the Royal Navy Inter Command Field Gun Competition and the Musical Drive of the King's Troop Royal Horse Artillery, the Tournament was establishing itself in the entertainment world again.

In his foreword to the 1959 programme, Marshal of the Royal Air Force Sir William Dickson, remarked that National Service was coming to an end in 1960. He noted the contribution that National Service men had made to the Tournament over the years. Going on to say that "National Service has created a close link between the public and the Forces, and this Royal Tournament is a great opportunity for the public to see their Armed Forces at close quarters".

EIGHT – TIME FOR CHANGE

On 22 June, the Tournament entered the 1960s, this was the latest date that the show had opened to the public since the 1920s (8 – 24 July 1926). Since the war, the show had established itself in June, usually opening in the first week, and running for a period of 17 days. An article in the *Portsmouth Evening News* on 23 June 1960, raised a question about the dates. It suggested that the Tournament could be run earlier in the year, saying, "Such a move, it is felt, would enable thousands more children to see this colourful spectacle, act as an incentive to recruiting, and, at the same time, assure the Tournament of improving the support which has been on the decline for some years".

Captain F.P. Baker RN (a member of the Tournament Committee) responded that "serious thought had been given to the suggestion, but if the Tournament was held at Easter, for instance, training of the men would present a problem. It would have to start before Christmas and that was unlikely to meet with general approval." These comments were in reference to the Field Gun Crew's, who's training began early in the new year in order to be ready for the Tournament in June. Other performers began rehearsing in the spring for their displays at the Tournament each summer.

28 - Royal Tournament Programme 1960

In the end, the dates of the Tournament shifted back rather than forward. From 1962 onwards the show opened (with a few exceptions) between 9 and 15 July, closing sometime between 27 July and 2 August. These dates usually straddled the end of the school term, providing an opportunity for school trips during the matinee performances early in the run and family outings towards the end. For some, their experience of seeing the Royal Tournament 'for real' included a train or coach journey with their classmates as an end of term treat. For others, it was about watching the show with family, often children, parents, and grandparents, all of whom enjoyed the experience for different reasons but enjoyed it none the less.

By the 1960s the post-war interest in the Armed Forces had declined and the audience numbers for the Tournament were reducing as well. However, it should be remembered that a full house at the Earls Court was around 12,000 visitors, over twice that of the Royal Albert Hall and five times the size of the London Palladium. Apart from the shift in dates, the Tournament Committee were reluctant to change, and as such the established format for the programme continued throughout the 60s.

Performances opened with the Mounted Competitions (Individual or Team Show Jumping and Sword, Lance & Revolver), giving a direct link back to the Islington days. Each performance ended with the Massed Bands. The programme usually included one or two physical training displays, a Drill Display, and an occasional Band from overseas.

The Band of the Queen's Own Nigerian Regiment took part in the 1960 show. Their display included a detachment from the regiment who sang on the march and performed traditional Nigerian dances. The Massed Military and Pipe Bands of the Brigade of Gurkhas also performed under the direction of Major J.P.C. Bailey. Another famous signature appeared in the 1960 programme, as the foreword was written by Admiral of the Fleet, The Earl Mountbatten of Burma.

From 1947, four crews had taken part in the Field Gun Competition each year. However, with reductions in the size of the Royal Navy following the Second World War, in 1956, Divisional Manning was replaced by Central Manning. Chatham became home to the reserve fleet. Following the 1960 Royal Tournament, Chatham withdrew from the Field Gun Competition, leaving three crews: Portsmouth, Devonport, and Air Command. The fastest time at this point stood at 3 mins 9 3/5 secs, set by Air Command in 1959.

The Parachute Regiment demonstrated an Airborne Assault in 1961. The arena was first shown as an RAF Airfield as troops and equipment were loaded for the mission. Then with the sound of an aircraft overhead, the audience looked towards the roof to see a wave of parachute troops make their decent to the Drop Zone. An anti-tank gun followed and was brought into action before the Paras left the arena to "rendezvous with the rest of the assault force."

The Royal Navy gave a flight deck demonstration in 1962, arming four Sea Vixen aircraft and preparing them for flight. The aircraft were launched from the flight deck (through the arena doors) with a specially produced film projected onto a screen showing the onward journey of the aircraft. The Royal Air Force produced a display entitled "Cavalcade of Flying" marking 50 years since the formation of the Royal Flying Corps, charting the story of flight from hot the air balloon to the jet age.

The Fort Henry Guard from Canada returned to the Tournament in 1963. The Massed Bands that year were drawn from the Royal Armoured Corps under the direction of Captain Trevor L. Sharpe of the Royal Tank Regiment. The Massed Bands were:

5th Royal Inniskilling Dragoon Guards
1st The Royal Dragoons
Royal Scots Greys (2nd Dragoons)
10th Royal Hussars (Prince of Wales's Own)
17th/21st Lancers
Royal Tank Regiment.

The music included 'Light Cavalry' (Suppe) and 'Marching Around the Shows' (arr. Duthoit) as well as 'Music for a Tournament' and 'Conquerer's All' both composed by Capt. Sharpe. The Household Cavalry and the Royal Armoured Corps produced a pageant "Horses to Horsepower" charting their history from mounted troops to armoured vehicles.

The Royal Navy display of 1964 was titled "Way Aloft", an 80 ft tall mast was assembled and rigged in the arena. The programme notes said, "The display sets out to reproduce, on a reduced scale, the mast training that all Junior new entries are required to perform during their initial period at the Training Schools." This mast used at Earls Court was about half the height of the one at H.M.S. Ganges. In the acknowledgements, thanks were given to Messrs. Accles and Pollock of Birmingham who constructed the mast and Bertram Mills Circus who "provided many ideas on the erection of the mast". The mast was manned by 21 Junior ratings.

1964 was also the tercentenary of the formation of the Royal Marines, the Massed Bands of HM Royal Marines marked the occasion by recreating the Beating Retreat which had been conducted earlier in the year to mark the birthday of their Captain General, HRH Prince Philip, The Duke of Edinburgh.

The Band and Dancers of the Fiji Military Forces took part in 1965. The programme notes said that "like all South Sea Islanders, the Fijians are naturally musical and nobody in the Band has received any formal musical education." The display also included traditional dances called Mekes. The Royal Air Force provided the Massed Bands Display under the direction of under the direction of Wing Commander J.L. Wallace. The display included 'The Queen's Colour' written by Wallace as well as popular film music; 'Flash, Bang, Wallop' (Heneker) from Half a Sixpence and 'Consider Yourself' (Bart) from Oliver!

29 - Royal Tournament Programme 1966

The Pakistan Frontier Constabulary visited in 1966, providing "A Display of Pathan Tribal Dancing & Drill with Pipe Band". The display team performed two traditional dances; "Khattak" and "Balbala/Gadwana" which had previously been performed before battle but were more ceremonial by the 1960s.

Unusually, there were two Massed Band displays in 1966. The Massed Bands and Bugles of the Light Infantry Brigade under the direction of Bandmaster R.A. Ridings of the King's Shropshire Light Infantry performed 'Queen and Prince' (Young) and 'Light Infantry' (Plater). The Massed Bands of the Royal Artillery was made up of; The Band of The Royal Artillery Band, The Royal Artillery Mounted Band (no longer mounted, but retained its traditional title), The Royal Artillery (BAOR[19]) Band, The Band of the Junior Leaders Regiment, Royal Artillery, and The Junior Musicians Troop, Royal Artillery. Under the direction of Captain R. Quinn, they provided the musical accompaniment to the display "Guns and Gunners – Then and Now" marking 250 years of the Royal Artillery.

The last day of the 1966 Tournament clashed with the World Cup Final at Wembley Stadium. Assistant Commentator (as he was at the time) Basil Reitz later recalled announcing that England had beaten West Germany to the audience at Earls Court.

The Band of the Jamaica Regiment promised to bring "Caribbean sunshine" to Earls Court in 1967, with their Band, Drums, and Dancers playing traditional Jamaican Airs and Calypsos'. The Massed Pipes & Drums of the Lowland and Highland Brigades also performed in 1967. Representing seven[20] of the eight Scottish Infantry Regiments of the time; Royal Scots (The Royal Regiment), The Royal Highland Fusiliers, The King's Own Scottish Borderers, The Cameronians (Scottish Rifles), The Black Watch (Royal Highland Regiment), Queen's Own Highlanders, and The Gordan Highlanders.

An Inter-Service Vehicle-Handling competition was staged at the 1967 Tournament to mark the 50th Anniversary of the Royal Society for the Prevention of Accidents (RoSPA). Teams were entered from the Royal Navy, Royal Marines, two from the Army, and two from the RAF. Each team consisted of two women and six men. In the first leg of each competition, the women drove Mini Minors around a course of obstacles before their male colleagues took their turn, driving Land Rovers with trailers "under combat conditions with additional hazards". Points were awarded for the fastest time for each section of the team (after penalties were awarded for any infringements of the competition rules).

The Second Battalion, Princess Patricia's Canadian Light Infantry took their turn at the Tournament in 1968. They were based in Germany at the time as part of Canada's NATO forces and provided a Drill Display for the Tournament. Another display: "The Royal Engineers – Past and Present" included the setting up of a Medium Girder Bridge in the centre of the arena, while small detachments of 'Sappers' recreated historical incidents

---

[19] British Army of the Rhine (BOAR)
[20] The Pipes & Drums of the Argyll and Sutherland Highlanders were serving with their Battalion in Aden

from their past. This included early aviation; balloons, man-lifting kites, and early aircraft. Musical support was provided by the Band of the Corps of Royal Engineers, Aldershot directed by Captain E.G. Horabin.

For the first time in 1968, the souvenir programme listed the "Occupants of the Royal Box". Since the very early days, the Royal Family had supported the Tournament, each successive Lord Mayor of London had also been a patron and had taken their turn to occupy the Royal Box. The list in 1968 also included The Rt. Hon. Denis Healey (Secretary of State for Defence), Admiral Sir Varyl Begg (First Sea Lord), General Sir Geoffrey Baker (Chief of General Staff), Air Chief Marshal Sir John Grady (Chief of the Air Staff), and Field Marshal The Viscount Montgomery of Alamein as well as H.R.H. The Princess Margaret, H.M. The Queen and H.R.H. The Duke of Edinburgh.. The tradition of listing the occupants of the Royal Box continued until the Last Run.

As the decade drew to a close, 3rd Bersaglieri Regiment from Italy took part in the Tournament, marking the 20th Anniversary of NATO. Bersaglieri means chosen marksman, they are known for their resistance to fatigue and swiftness of movement. The display brought together the fast-moving Fanfara trumpeters and gymnasts. The Royal Canadian Mounted Police returned in 1969 to perform their Musical Ride.

30 - Royal Tournament Programme 1969

The Royal Marines put a 'new spin' on their Commando Raid, in this scenario "Earthquake 69", they teamed up with detachment from H.M.S. Blake to demonstrate a humanitarian mission. The Commando's scaled the walls of the fictitious Mediterranean island walled city of "Juno" which had been struck by a devastating earthquake. Having climbed into the ruined city, they went on to extract the casualties who were then moved by helicopter to receive treatment.

The Massed Bands of the Royal Armoured Corps returned in 1969, performing popular tunes such as 'Boom Bang-a-Bang[21]' (Moorhouse) and 'Chitty Chitty Bang Bang' (Sherman) under the direction of Captain Clifford V. Wright of the Rhine Staff Band, Royal Tank Regiment

The Royal Brunei Malay Regiment took part in the 1970 Tournament. They provided a drill display, accompanied by their Regimental Band. The troops were in traditional dress, carrying Royal Ceremonial Umbrella, which were part of the court regalia. The senior officers of state from Brunei, known as "Wazir," were represented in the arena by members of the Regiment. They departed the arena in a ceremonial boat known as a "Peraha" with an escort carrying traditional spears.

The Massed Bands of the RAF closed each performance in 1970 under the direction of Wing Commander R.E.C. Davies. In another contemporary programme, they performed 'Hey Look me Over' (Coleman arr. Martindale) from the 1960 Broadway musical Wildcat, 'Lara's Theme' (Maurice Jarre arr. Martindale) from the popular film Doctor Zhivago (1965), and the main theme from the film 'Paint Your Wagon' (Loewe arr. Martindale) which had been released in January 1970.

The Massed Bands and Bugles of the Light Division (formed on 1 July 1968) also performed in 1970. Their musical programme included: 'Lily the Pink' (Pannel), 'On the Square' (Mancini), and 'Light Infantry' (Plater) under the Direction of Bandmaster J.C. Mutlow of The Royal Green Jackets.

The Gurkhas provided two displays in 1971. In the first display The Band of the Brigade of Gurkhas (2nd King Edward VII's Own Gurkha Rifles) and The Bugles of 2nd King Edward VII's Own Gurkha Rifles (The Sirmoor Rifles) performed at the Rifle Regiment's 140 paces per minute before pausing for a static display which included 'Can't Buy Me Love' (Lennon & McCartney arr. Bentley). They were then joined by the display team who performed a Kukri Dance using the Gurkha's traditional weapon. Later in the programme, the display team returned to conduct a "Jungle Attack."

Five of the eight Regiments of the Scottish Division provided Pipes & Drums for the display in 1971. The Massed Bands of The Royal Marines also performed the ceremony of Beating Retreat as part of their display, the

[21] Performed by Lulu at the Eurovision Song Contest 1969

programme included 'Semper Fidelis' (Sousa), 'Golden Spurs' (Rhodes), and 'Eagle Squadron' (Alford).

Basil Reitz was promoted from the Assistant to Commentator in 1972, Dr J.P.M Reid, stepped down from the role following the 1971 Tournament.

The Massed Bands of the Infantry performed in 1972 representing, The Royal Regiment of Fusiliers, The King's Regiment, The Devonshire and Dorset Regiment, and The Duke of Wellington's Regiment. The programme included 'The Trombone King' (R.C. King), 'El Capitan' (Sousa), and 'Bugler's Holiday' (Leroy Anderson).

The Singapore Armed Forces took part in the 1972 Tournament, performing traditional Lion, Flag, and Frog Dances. The RAF Police Dogs and the Queen's Colour Squadron of the RAF also appeared.

Two overseas acts took part in 1973; The Charanga of the Portuguese Republican National Guard provided an equine display with their mounted band. The Band of the Royal Barbados Police performed music including 'Come Listen to the Band' (Monckton), 'Island in the Sun' (Burgie), and 'West Indian Boys are Marching' (arr. Cave). They were directed by Mr Prince Albert Cave, who was born in Barbados and enlisted in the Band as a Cadet in 1936. He went on to train at the Royal Military School of Music at Kneller Hall before returning home to take up the position of Director of Music.

The Bands, Pipes, Bugles, Drums and Dancers of the Royal Irish Rangers also performed in 1973. Their programme included traditional Irish music 'St. Patrick's Day', 'Back to Donegal', and 'Sligo'. 42 Commando Royal Marines conducted an "Arctic Ambush" and the Royal Air Force gave a demonstration of parachute training. The Massed Bands of the RAF closed the show with a display which included 'Eagle Squadron' (K. Alford), 'Fame and Glory' (A.E. Matt), and 'The Dambusters' (Eric Coats).

The formula for the Tournament, established following the move to Earls Court in 1950 had changed little in over two decades. It was becoming stale; the show had failed to move with the times.

NINE – REIMAGINATION

To reimagine something is to 'imagine again' or in a 'different way.' I'm not sure that this term was in common use in the UK in the 1970s or if the person who is about to enter our story would have used it. But nevertheless, it describes exactly what he did.

The post-war popularity of the Royal Tournament had declined, the audience numbers had dwindled from the mid-fifties onwards. Each year the show followed a similar formula, to some extent audiences started to attend every other year or less frequently without feeling that they were missing anything. In 1973 the first (and only) Producer was appointed by the Royal Tournament Committee, Captain Micheal Parker who had recently left the Queen's Own Hussars, he was now an Auxiliary Emergency Reserve (AER).

Major Sir Michael Parker

Born at Fulmer Chase Maternity Hospital near Gerrards Cross, Buckinghamshire on 21 September 1941. Michael was Commissioned into the Queen's Own Hussars, serving as a Troop Leader, Gunnery Instructor, and Adjutant.

While stationed in Germany, he began staging Mess Functions as well as Military events, including the Berlin Tattoo. He was appointed as the Producer of the Royal Tournament in 1973, producing the show from 1974 to 1999.

He also masterminded the Queen's Jubilee celebrations in 1977 and 2022 as well as the 100th Birthday Pageant for the Queen Mother in 2000.

He produced spectacular events in the UK and oversees including the Edinburgh Tattoo, the Royal Military Tattoo 2000, and QM100.

In his biography, "It's all going Terribly Wrong" Micheal Parker said of the Tournament "gradually over the years the show had lost its unique appeal. It had failed to keep up with the times and from being the only way to see exciting live entertainment it became just one of many." The Tournament had been at the forefront of live entertainment, creating new experiences to delight and surprise audiences for decades but it's fair to say that it had been resting on its laurels for some time. The culture of "we've always done it this way" had crept in to the organising committee, but fortunately change was coming.

Colonel B. L. Gunnell, OBE, MC had taken over the position of Vice-Chairman[22] of the Royal Tournament in 1964. As Vice-Chair, he was responsible for the day to day running of the small permanent staff and overseeing the planning and delivery of each Tournament. Col. Gunnell was due to retire after the 1973 show, his successor was named as Colonel A.H.N (Dan) Reade. He began shadowing the role during the 1973 Tournament.

Col Arthur Harold Newmarch "Dan" Reade had been the 2nd in command of the Queen's Own Hussars and knew Micheal Parker well. Parker had organised spectacular pageants and reenactments as part of the Regimental Mess Functions while based in Germany. Dan Reade invited Michal Parker to the final night of the 1973 Royal Tournament. Parker recalled that "The evening started with a mean fanfare by about ten trumpets" going on to say "The show then staggered from act to act. All were quite unmemorable except for the King's Troop, Royal Horse Artillery who were immaculate as usual, and the Royal Navy Field Gun Competition which was as baffling as usual".

Over a drink following the performance Dan Reade asked Micheal what he thought of the show saying, "What I mean is – could you do any better?" Micheal's response was "I certainly couldn't do any worse!" Col Reade joined the staff of the Tournament as Director[23] and Capt. Parker as Producer, both new roles which would shape the next stage of the show's history. In modern terms, the Director was responsible for the 'Business Management' of the Tournament and the Producer had responsibility for the 'Creative Direction.'

Both Col. Reade and Capt. Parker set about trying to help the Tournament catch up with the times, Reade in the administration and box office, and Parker in the Arena. Both met with resistance! The Tournament Committee were what we would now describe as 'change resistant' and 'risk averse.'

From a production point of view, there were two settings for the arena lighting; 'on' or 'off', and the order of the displays still changed from performance to performance. There was a large board on each side of the arena at the balcony level of Earls Court showing the order of the

---

[22] The position of Chairman was taken up by each successive Major-General Commanding the Household Brigade and General Officer Commanding London District (as the role was known in 1964).

[23] From an organising committee point of view, also Vice Chairman.

displays and the number of the current display so that the audience could follow in their programme. Parker was keen to change both (amongst other elements of the Tournament), but he was beginning to realise that it wasn't going to happen overnight!

A massed bands display had closed the show at each performance for many years, the three services providing massed bands in rotation; Royal Marines (for the Navy), followed by Massed Army Bands (provided by the Infantry, Artillery, Armoured Corps or Light Infantry) the next year, and the Massed Royal Air Force Bands after that.

The bands themselves had an established routine and were reluctant to do anything different. They only performed once in each performance and weren't keen to increase this. Parker persuaded (over the course of a few 'good lunches', I'm told) the Director of Music of HM Royal Marines, Lt Col. Paul Neville that it would be a good idea to stage a proper Finale to end the show in 1974 (a Navy year), in addition to the massed bands display. A new piece of music was commissioned (to be the naval equivalent of the 1812 Overture) for this purpose.

Former Royal Marines Bandsman Albert Elms, who had written popular television themes such as 'The Adventures of Robin Hood', 'The Champions', and 'The Prisoner', took on the commission. He composed 'The Battle of Trafalgar' which was performed by the 300 strong, Massed Bands of HM Royal Marines for the finale. The bands formed up in the centre of the arena and two, 80 ft high replica ships of the British and French Navies were lowered from the ceiling on either side of the Massed bands and engaged in battle as new work was performed.

A 'record-breaking' White Ensign was also created to be unfurled from the ceiling at the climax of the finale, it measured 100 ft x 60 ft and incorporated a 36 ft x 18 ft Union Flag (loaned from the Palace of Westminster). After a few 'teething problems' during the rehearsals, the finale was coming together, the Massed Bands were immaculate as always, the ships were being lowered into place at the correct time and the 'pyrotechnics' for the naval battle were being discharged (safely). Parker then decided to augment the finale sequence with a Nelson Tableau, made up of Naval Ratings dressed as Nelson, Hardy, a Surgeon, and a few sailors. At short notice, he recruited the cast from the RN Display Team, had costumes delivered to Earls Court, and rehearsed the addition. This was in the spirit of one of his 'Rules' that he worked by this one being

"If you're 100% certain that an event is going to work perfectly, you're not being ambitions enough".

Lieutenant Colonel A. J. Preston (Jumbo) had taken over the role of Arena Master in 1960 (and would remain in post until 1980). Formerly of the 9th/12th Lancers and by now retired, he lived in Majorca for most of the year and returned to London each summer for the Tournament. The Arena Master role was first carried out by Capt. Dann (although known as the Steward of the Arena back at Islington), he not only called forward the performers from the waiting area to enter the arena for their display or competition but also in the days before a public address system, made the arena announcements. It would be fair to say that Capt. Dann 'ran the show'. His successors as Stewards of the Arena, Officers in Charge of the Arena, and later Arena Master fulfilled similar roles. It's therefore possible to see why Lt Col. Jumbo may not have seen eye-to-eye with the new Producer (particularly one only holding the rank of Captain).

Jumbo had been in post for over a decade and the Earls Court Team would only take direction from him. However, with some persuasion Capt. Parker won them over and they, somewhat reluctantly, removed the boards listing the order of the acts from the balcony. Paving the way for the order of the acts to be the same for each performance.

Little by little, the 'reimagination' was starting to take shape. Another key change brought in by Capt. Parker was the addition of a painted backcloth, specifically designed by Parker to fit with the theme of the Tournament each year. Previously, the 'Scenery' as it was acknowledged in the souvenir programme was provided by Earls Court Ltd. It usually took the form of a Fort or a Cliff for the Royal Marines to assault. Capt. Parker's vision was that the backcloth would be an integral part of the performance. His original artwork[24] was painted on boards 24 in x 8 in and scaled up to 240 ft x 80 ft for the Earls Court arena.

The first backcloth design incorporated a Naval Crown, anchors, and ramrods. It was 100 ft wide (the width of the arena, later backcloths extended to the back of the stalls and even to the depth of the balcony

[24] Following his death in 2022, the original artwork for all his Royal Tournament designs were handed over to The Museum of The Queen's Royal Hussars and are now on display in the Parker Gallery at the museum in Warwick.

31 - The first specifically designed Backcloth for the 1974 Tournament, artwork by Micheal Parker

on a few occasions) and 80 ft high. It was painted by Peter Davidson of Barrett Brothers (LONDON) Ltd, the Earls Court Stand Fitting Company. This was the first time that Peter had been requested to paint anything other than the usual landscape, castle, or cliff face for the Tournament. He set out the canvas on the rear carpark at Earls Court and painted using domestic brooms and drums of paint. The end product was excellent and set a precedent for future backcloths.

32 - Royal Tournament Programme Cover 1974

A group of drummers and dancers from the Sri Lanka Police Reserve performed at the 1974 Tournament. This included a Hewisi Band playing traditional Sri Lankan music, 21 drummers and acrobatic dancers.

Following the Tournament, the group stayed on in the UK, performing at the Colchester and Edinburgh Tattoos.

The photograph on the front cover of the Souvenir Programme in 1974 was taken during a professional photo shoot onboard H.M.S. Victory in Portsmouth. It featured a 32-pounder cannon and serving members of the Royal Navy in Trafalgar Dress. The impactful image was used in on posters to promote the show. A separate photo from the shoot was used for the cover of the 1981 programme.

33 - Design of the 1975 Backcloth by Maj Micheal Parker

The Army was the lead service in 1975, the theme for the finale was the "Retreat from Moscow". The Massed Bands of the Royal Armoured Corps; The Royal Scots Dragoon Guards, 4th/7th Royal Dragoon Guards, The Queen's Own Hussars, The Royal Hussars, The 13th/18th Royal Hussars, 14th/20th King's Hussars, 16th/5th The Queen's Royal Lancers, and the Royal Tank Regiment all appeared in the finale in period costume. The Director of Music of the Cambrai Staff Band, Royal Tank Regiment, Captain Brian Keeling appearing on horseback dressed as Napoleon. The music included: 'Song of the Plains', 'Marseillaise', 'St. Peter's Prayer', 'Napoleon's Retreat', and '1812 Overture'. The backcloth depicted the Moscow skyline as viewed from outside the city walls. For the majority of each performance, a huge British Army symbol (crossed swords, crown, and lion) featured on the centre of the backcloth on a 'flap' which was folded back to reveal the full skyline for the finale.

The Pipes & Drums of the Australian States Police Force and The Marine Band of the Royal Netherlands Navy also performed in 1975. In their display, the Royal Marines took part in 'Operation Polar Bear', assaulting a "rocky foreshore somewhere in North Norway" to rescue a "diplomat and his wife who had been captured by an invasion force". Two Scorpion vehicles from "A" Squadron, The Blues and Royals provided support for the Marines.

The lead service in 1976 was the Royal Air Force, the finale theme was the Great War, following the progression of warfare from the stalemate of the trenches, through the advent of the Tank to the birth of the Royal Air Force. The backcloth showed an RAF Eagle over a scarred battlefield landscape. The finale included scale models of German and British First World War Aircraft (made by the Royal Air Force Model Aircraft Society) engaged in a Dog Fight above the Arena and replica Mark IV Tank (made by Apprentices of 30 Command Workshops, REME).

The RAF demonstrated the deployment of a Harrier in their display "Rapid Response" which culminated in the simulated vertical take-off of the aircraft. The Royal Marines Physical Training Wing from the Depot at Deal gave a demonstration of Martial Arts and the Royal Artillery Motor Cycle Display Team gave their first display at the Tournament in 1976.

34 - King's Toop RHA Officer and Trumpeter at the 1999 Royal Tournament

The Musical Drive had been thrilling audiences since the first display by D Battery, Royal Horse Artillery at Islington in 1896. Michael Parker had been making suggestions as to how the drive could be improved further (without any luck) since 1974. With the arrival of Major Mike Webster as the new Commanding Officer in 1976, there was an opportunity to make changes. Maj. Webster was keen to do anything which would improve the Drive. Two changes were accepted.

1. An Officer and Trumpeter would be made available for each performance. Their role would be to enter the darkened arena first (under spotlight) and announce the arrival of the musical drive with a trumpet call.
2. At the end of each Musical Drive, two guns would leave the arena. The remaining four would be brought into action, individually and then all together. Two-ounce charges were created for firing indoors.

These additions added to the drama of the display and are both still part of the Musical Drive today.

35 - Design for the Backcloth of the 1977 Royal Tournament by Maj Micheal Parker

The Royal Navy were the lead service for the Queen's Silver Jubilee Tournament in 1977. Micheal Parker (recently promoted to Major) had originally planned to recreate an element of the Jubilee Fleet Review for the finale. Walkways suspended 60 ft above the arena in the outline of a ship were to be manned by naval ratings. However, the agreement to access Earls Court two weeks earlier than usual to set this up was withdrawn at short notice and an alternative finale had to be found. A new 80 ft mast was built to fit into Earls Court. This was an evolution of the "Way Aloft" display by the Royal Navy at the 1964 Tournament. Music for the finale was provided by the Massed Bands of HM Royal Marines including 'Heart of Oak', 'Rule Britannia', 'Shenandoah', and 'Sunset'. In a celebration of the

Jubilee year, the Australian Army Band Corps and The British Columbia Beefeater Band also travelled to London to take part in the Tournament.

Following the tradition of overseas performers, the Royal Hong King Police Band performed at the 1978 Tournament. The Pipes & Drums of the 6th Queen Elizabeth's Own Gurkha Rifles also took part along with the Massed Bands of the Infantry.

36 - The 1978 Finale: Waterloo – Wellington's Victory

The finale had two phases, the first was "Waterloo – Wellington's Victory", including the Massed Bands as well as Horsemen from the Household Cavalry and The King's Troop RHA. The second phase marked the novocentenary (900th Anniversary) of the Tower of London (linked to Wellington as he was a previous Constable of the Tower) with a recreation of the Ceremony of the Keys. Maj Parker had produced a similar display for the Berlin Tattoo, the backcloth showed the Tower of London (with some elements brought over from Berlin with a view to keeping costs down) surrounded by a 'Garter Arch' including the Royal motto 'Honi soit qui mal y pense' ('Evil to him who evil thinks') and a heraldic Lion and Unicorn.

The backcloth was used again in 1979, and the Ceremony of the Keys[25] was once again incorporated into the Finale. Although there was no new backcloth this year, there was new technology. The first phase of the Finale was "The Story of Flight told with Music and Lasers." The musical programme included: 'Fanfare for the Common Man', 'Stars and Stripes Forever', 'Aces High', 'The Dambusters', and 'Mars'.

With the introduction of lasers, the Tournament was once again at the forefront of entertainment technology as the 1970s drew to a close. Col. Reade and Maj. Parker had both played their part in putting the Tournament back onto a strong footing. Public relations, marketing, and advertising advisors had all been engaged to raise the profile of the show, audience numbers were increasing, and the BBC Television Coverage had also been reinvigorated. The reimagination of the Tournament was taking shape and was impacting positively, but there was still more to do.

[25] The 2nd Battalion Scots Guards and Yeoman Warders had recreated the ceremony at Olympia in 1948

TEN – CENTENARY

On 9 July 1980, the Centenary Tournament opened at Earls Court. Since the first Grand Military Tournament and Assault-at-Arms was staged at Islington in 1880, the motorcar had been invented and rolled out to the masses, aviators had flown for the first time, fought dogfights, gone supersonic, and travelled into space, there had been two global conflicts, and the world was entering the Digital Age. There had been a considerable amount of change in that 100-year timeframe (perhaps more than any other in history) but the Royal Tournament was still fondly held in the hearts of the British public. The appeal was cross-generational; children, parents, and grandparents all enjoyed their experience at the Tournament. In addition to family groups, the Tournament was attracting coach parties from across the country as well as the fashionable London 'after work crowd,' there was something for everyone.

37 - Design of the Centenary Tournament Backcloth by Maj Micheal Parker

The 1980 Tournament opened with the fanfare 'Centenary' played by the State Trumpeters and Drumhorses of the Household Cavalry, and the Band of the Irish Guards. Then followed the Royal Navy Field Gun Competition and Musical Drive of the King's Troop RHA. A Combined Services Physical Training Display included elements from earlier Tournaments such as Bayonet Exercise and Fencing, followed by maze marching, trampoline, and high horse displays. There was also an inter-service motor-cycle competition and displays from the King's Squad Royal Marines, RAF Police Dogs and a Quadrille from the Household Cavalry. The overseas act came from the Kenya Army Band and Dancers. This was a truly tri-service Royal Tournament, the Massed Bands were drawn from Band of HM Royal Marines, Band of the Irish Guards, and Central Band of the Royal Air Force. The flags of the three services were suspended from the ceiling, unfurling as the respective band marched into the arena. The backcloth was painted with a huge Royal Standard, Garter Arch, and heraldic Lion and Unicorn again.

38 - Royal Tournament 1880-1980, A Pictorial History by Lord Chalfont

Also in 1980, Robert Ornbo and Roger Straker from Theatre Projects were brought in to review the arena lighting. In 1974, there had been twelve light fittings suspended slightly above the balcony level, which glowed white/amber across the whole arena, they couldn't be independently switched off to either highlight or hide any part of the arena floor. This had moved on slightly with the help of Rank Strand Electric Ltd but was still not fit for purpose. The proposal from Theatre Projects for a modern lighting rig was expensive, the BBC had been filming the Tournament for many years and had complained about the poor lighting for some time, they were invited to 'contribute' to the additional lighting cost, which they reluctantly did. This improved the live experience for the Earls Court audience and the quality of the output for the BBC television coverage.

To mark the Centenary, Lord Chalfont produced a History of the Royal Tournament. This was the first history of the Tournament to be published since the 1950s.

The grand finale was "A Cavalcade of the Royal Tournament during the past one hundred years", with an appropriately patriotic soundtrack from the tri-service Massed Bands: 'Imperial Echoes' (Saffroni), 'Pomp and Circumstance No. 4' (Elgar), 'Crown Imperial' Walton, and 'Sunset' (Green). The National Anthem followed, and the march-off music was 'Famous songs of the British Isles' (Dunn) and the ever popular 'The Army, the Navy and the Air Force' (arr Cole). The Centenary Tournament had acknowledged the rich history of the Royal Tournament and raised the bar again in terms of the production of the show.

Following the 1980 show, Col. Dan Reade announced his intention to retire as the Director of the Tournament following the 1981 Tournament. Colonel Iain Ferguson, late Scots Guards was appointed as his replacement, shadowing Col. Reade over the course of the 1981 Tournament before assuming control completely.

Lt. Col. Jumbo Preston also stood down after the 1980 Tournament having served 20 years as Arena Master. Maj. Parker was concerned about having another Officer take on the Arena Master role, on his other projects this was a Senior NCO role, usually a Warrant Officer. However, on the recommendation of the new Director Col. Ferguson,, another officer was appointed. Major George Douglas took on the role in time for the 1981 Tournament.

Colonel Iain Ferguson

Following a career with the Scots Guards, retiring as Colonel, Iain Ferguson was appointed as the Director of the Royal Tournament in 1981.

He was responsible for overseeing the Business Management of the Tournament and leading the small permanent staff based at Horse Guards (later Wellington Barracks).

Margaret Ferguson (Iain's wife) also became involved with the Tournament, overseeing the running of the Royal Box. A keen flower arranger she organised a Flower Show in 1995 to celebrate the Centenary of Westminster Cathedral.

Following the tri-Service Centenary Tournament, the rotation of the lead service was resumed with the Royal Navy in 1981. The Fanfare was replaced by an 'Opening' for the first time. The theme of the 1981 Tournament was the Battle of Trafalgar but this time a 'a golden thread' was weaved through the whole performance. Not every act, but a handful of displays were linked to the theme (a tactic which would be employed successfully again and again in later years).

Admiral Lord Nelson joined the fleet during the opening, later the Royal Navy Display Team (in Trafalgar dress) demonstrated of 32 Pounder Gun Drill using a replica gun

Major George Douglas

George McDonald-Douglas joined the Grenadier Guards at the age of 18 in 1943. Following the War, he transferred to the Royal Army Service Corps (later Royal Corps of Transport). He retired from the Army in 1977.

He was appointed as the Arena Master of the Royal Tournament in 1981, a position which he held until the Last Run in 1999. He was described in an article by Soldier Magazine as "The 'Phantom' who made the arena run like clockwork.

from Victory, the display team returned again for a window ladder display and at the end of the performance for the Grand Finale. The backcloth included a 3D model of H.M.S. Victory as well as the stern of the French Flagship both with firing cannons!

39 - Design of the 1981 Backcloth by Maj Micheal Parker

* * *

A new marketing initiative was launched in 1981 to engage with the younger members of the audience. The Royal Tournament Brigade was open to anyone aged between 5 and 18, they joined as a Cadet and were issued with a certificate (signed by the GOC London District, the Chairman of the Tournament), a badge, and membership card. New members (often their parents for the younger ones) would choose which of the Armed Forces they were most interested in, each year that they attended the Tournament (and remembered their membership card) they would progress through the ranks of their chosen service (Cadet to Admiral, Field Marshal or Marshal of the RAF).

The (very clever) marketing element came in the form of the newsletters which were delivered to the members in the post each spring. These included 'inside information' for the Brigade Members about the upcoming Tournament along with a special booking form to order tickets. The idea being that the young members would then encourage their parents (or grandparents) to book tickets. As a loyalty scheme it was extremely successful, the members would report to the Brigade Stand year after year to have their cards stamped. I wrote the content for the Royal Tournament Brigade newsletters for a few years in the 1990s and had the pleasure of meeting hundreds of members of the Royal Tournament Brigade at the stand alongside Angelique Kelly, who also manned the stand for many years.

*   *   *

1982 was an Army Year, the finale was once again "The Retreat from Moscow", incorporating the 1812 Overture with the Guns of the King's Troop RHA and Horsemen from the Household Cavalry taking part alongside the Army Massed Bands. The backcloth depicted another view of Moscow, with a section in the middle which opened up to reveal a cliff for the Royal Marines to assault. A new Fanfare 'Tradition' was written for the show by Major Derek Kimberley, Director of Music, Band of The Grenadier Guards. The fanfare began with an 18th Century Band (played by the Band of the Household Cavalry in period uniform) and showed the evolution of Military Bands to the 1980s with variations on 'British Grenadiers'.

The major change in 1982, however, was in the way the performance was structured. Earls Court had been resistant to the idea of an interval for many years but had finally agreed. The Royal Navy Field Gun competition traditionally appeared early in each performance, with the house band playing during the 'lynch in' of the walls and ramps, which took approximately 15 minutes. With the updated structure, this activity could now take place during the Interval, allowing an opportunity to watch for those who wanted to and for those who didn't, to visit the conveniences, concession stands, and static displays behind the seating.

To balance the programme, the Musical Drive was moved forward to be the second display of the show, with the Massed Bands closing the first half of the performance. The Royal Navy Field Gun Competition opened the second half. The Finale was by now established as the climax of the show. This was the format that Maj. Parker had wanted to put in place since taking over as Producer eight years earlier. It would form the model for the Royal Tournament (and many other Tattoo's) from this point onwards.

The 1983 theme was "The Battle of Britain" with the Royal Air Force as the lead service. The backcloth depicted St Paul's Cathedral along with a series of buildings and houses, some of which 'collapsed' during the opening of the performance as though they had been bombed during an Air Raid. The arena was then filled with vintage vehicles including a 1940s London Bus and appliances from the Volunteer Fire Preservation Society. The Finale of the show was a Victory Parade including community singing (led by Dame Vera Lynn at some performances).

The Royal Air Force Motor Sport Association competed in a 'Motor and Motorcycle Competition' in 1983. There had been interservice vehicle handling competitions in previous years, but this was the first fully RAF display. The competing teams from Strike Command and Support Command first tested their driving skills in Mini Metro cars. The teams then changed the engines before completing another lap! The drivers then handed over to two motorcyclists who raced over obstacles to the finish line.

The format of the Souvenir Programme had changed little since the 1910s, the size had varied from modern A5 to A4, stapled with a central fold. In 1983 this changed to an A4 Perfect Bound, glossy, book or show guide format. The new format stretched to more than 100 full colour pages, enabling the many sponsors who were now supporting the show to be acknowledged with full page adverts.

This new format also included the first published layout drawing of the Royal Tournament exhibition area. Static displays had been a part of the Tournament in the Olympia days, housed in the National Hall. The vast space at Earls Court allowed for considerably more exhibition space (approx. 7,500 m^2 by 1999). The layout drawings which began to appear in the programme helped to orientate visitors. The lead service would take the exhibition space at the Warwick Road Entrance, the other two services would setup their display in the West Brompton and Philbeach sides behind the stalls.

The static displays provided an opportunity for visitors (of all ages) to meet members of the Armed Forces in person, veterans would compare notes of their service experience with the current serving generation and youngsters had an opportunity to ask what life in the forces was really like. The interaction between the public and their Armed Forces was a key part of the Tournament.

Over the years, visitors had an opportunity to view modern equipment at close quarters, sitting in the cockpit of a fighter jet or helicopter, climbing onboard a rigid raider or military vehicle. Assault Courses and hands on activities were always popular, younger visitors had an opportunity to 'Join the Army for 10 minutes', leaving with a souvenir button as a memento of the experience. There were always give aways on the stands too; posters, paper hats, souvenir bugs, and various stickers with messages such as 'future pilot' or 'I've met the Royal Marines.'

The Royal Navy took the lead again in 1984, the arena was turned into the Flight Deck of H.M.S. Ark Royal for the opening of the show. The backcloth was painted with a view of the aircraft carrier island and ski jump, a model sea harrier accelerated down the arena during the opening. As it exited through the arena doors a projector was switched on to show the aircraft taking off for a dawn patrol. The theme was "A Day in the Life of a Naval Officer," with a script written by Rosemary Anne Sisson. The show ending with the sunset ceremony as the finale, complete with mast manning and lowering of the White Ensign at dusk. Following the 1984 Tournament, £55,000[26] was donated to Armed Forces Charities, to this point the Tournament had donated almost £2 Million to charity.

Rosemary Anne Sisson

Rosemary was born in Enfield, Middlesex and attended Cheltenham Ladies' College before studying English at University College London. Her studies were interrupted during the Second World War when served in the Royal Observer Corps before returning to complete her degree. She taught English Literature at the University of Wisconsin before returning to Britain to lecture at UCL and Birmingham University.

She went on to write for period dramas such as Upstairs Downstairs (ITV) and The Six Wives of Henry VIII (BBC). Rosemary produced natural dialogue, Micheal Parker commissioned her to script characters and narration for the Royal Tournament and many other productions including the Royal Military Tattoo 2000.

* * *

The 1985 Royal Tournament was 'launched' on Thursday 17 January. For what appears to be the first (and only) time, the Royal Tournament Committee organised a separate event to promote the Tournament itself. It was titled "The 300th Anniversary Tribute to the Great British Regiments" and was staged at the Royal Albert Hall in the presence of Her Majesty Queen Elizabeth the Queen Mother. The narrative for the concert began with the Monmouth Rebellion in 1685 during the reign of James II, following the fortunes of the Regiments raised to subdue the rebellion (and their successors) up to 1985.

In his Forward to the concert programme, Major General James Eyre, mentioned that the 1984 Royal Tournament had reached 86% capacity and said that the aim was to increase on this at Earls Court later in the year.

[26] Equivalent to £175,000 in 2025

He also welcomed the many guests in the audience at the concert "from the press, Television, Radio, and other fields of public information" and reminded them to help achieve the objective by promoting the Tournament.

* * *

Mervyn Harridence

Mervyn Harridence had been a part of the Colchester theatre scene for many years, involved in productions of 'The Cherry Orchard' and 'The Most Happy Fella' He went on to become a talented scenic artist.

He created a 230 ft Rainbow and crock of gold for the Ideal Home Exhibition in 1985. Later that year, he took on the role of painter for the Royal Tournament backcloth. Mervyn painted the backcloths, designed by Maj Parker, from 1985 to 1996.

He also produced various props for the show including the Leonardo da Vinci Flying Machine and an inflatable submarine.

The backcloth designs were becoming more complex each year. In 1985 the Tournament marked the 300th Anniversary of the successor Regiments of those founded in 1685 to fight the Monmouth Rebellion. The centrepiece was a huge replica of a Grenadier Guards Side Drum which was raised on winches to reveal the arena doors. Behind the drum were the colours, guidons, and standards of the Regiments in 1985. Mervyn Harridence took over as the painter of the backcloth in 1985.

A dragon, created by 14 Field Workshop REME (Berlin), was flown over from Germany for the opening of the show, it was mounted on a Land Rover, breathed smoke, and had red glowing eyes! A young Life Guards officer by the name of Captain James Hewitt fought the dragon as St George twice a day for the duration of the Tournament. He also led a Cavalry Charge against an Infantry Square formed of Army Cadet Force in period uniforms of various era.

For the 1986 Tournament (an RAF year) Maj. Parker had designed a space themed backcloth. It was based on the view from the inside of the Space Shuttle looking out into space. Projection screens behind the gauze windows and a circular video screen were planned to show images of flight and space. However, this original design was scrapped following the Space Shuttle Challenger disaster on 28 January. A second design was produced with star cloth and the circular video screen, surrounded by clouds. This was reworked to become the final design which was used in the show. It included a central RAF Crest with six RAF flags and Colours above a World War Two era runway. A real Spitfire (minus the engine) was suspended over the arena doors, as if overflying the airfield.

The theme was "The Story of Flight", a circular lighting rig was lowered to the floor of the arena for the opening. The countdown from ten to one was projected onto the backcloth using lasers, the smoke, lighting, and sound effects gave a convincing impression of a rocket launch before the Massed Bands of the RAF entered the arena.

The circular rig appeared again in the finale with an inflatable globe suspended above it. The Massed Bands played an arrangement of the 'Planet Suite' by Holst, the lighting of the globe changing to give the impression of each of the planets.

Since 1969 Major R.A.G. "Rags" Courage had been the PR Officer for the Armed Forces at the Royal Tournament. During his tenure he had bridged the tricky gap between the military and civilian worlds, building strong relationships with the Press, TV, and Radio journalists who were sent to the Press Launch or performances at Earls Court, he ensured that they were looked after and encouraged that they portrayed the Tournament in a positive light. He retired after 17 years in the role following the 1986 run. As with many of the Royal Tournament Team, he returned in a voluntary role of Steward of the Royal Enclosure.

The theme for 1987 was "Birth of the British Navy – The First Ark Royal in 1587". The backcloth was the most complex to date, featuring a 16th Century Map of the Known World, it had a 200ft wide image of Neptune painted into it with ultraviolet paint which was revealed when the UV lighting was switched on. A three-dimensional Naval Crown rose from above the arena doors to the top of the backcloth during the opening sequence where it became part of the Lord High Admirals Badge. The centre of the badge surrounded by gold twisted rope, changed during the performance to show different historic ships: Golden Hind, H.M.S. Victory, a modern battleship and an aircraft carrier as well as an ornate compass.

The second half of the show followed the progress of a 1987 Royal Navy Task Force, setting sail, scrambling their aircraft, and entering into action with film from the Navy projected onto the Centre of the backcloth. The finale was the Coronation Fleet Review for King George V in 1911, with a modern-day ships company manning the rail and cheering the ship followed by mast manning.

> **Lieutenant Colonel Roy Stockwell**
>
> Lt Col Stockwell served for 26 years in The King's African Rifles (KAR), commanding 6th KAR in Tanganyika (Tanzania) from 1959 – 1963. After leaving the Army he returned home, taking on the role of Box Office Manager for the Tournament in 1969.
>
> The Box office was run by a tri-service team until the late 1970s when it was handed over to Earls Court to reduce the military manpower required. Lt Col Stockwell was then appointed as the Assistant Secretary, responsible for putting together the Souvenir Programme each year and keeping the archive.

A new addition to the Royal Tournament also arrived in 1987 in the form of a symbol depicting the three services. The Hippocamp had a horse's head, winged body, and a fish's tail. Lieutenant Colonel Roy Stockwell (Box Office Manager 1969 - 79, Assistant Secretary of the Royal Tournament 1980 – 84) came across a drawing of a Hippocamp at the Naval Museum at Greenwich. The mythological creatures which drew the chariot of Neptune, God of the sea. Described in the 1987 programme as "Powerful on land, across oceans and throughout the skies, this symbol of the Royal Tournament is truly representative of those who take part in the show each year". 150 Hippocamp models were made each year from 1987 to 1999 and were presented to leading participants by the Director as a "thank you" for their involvement. In the first year they were made in silver and brass and were mounted on a marble base, in the following years they were made in Fine China by Wedgwood, Royal Worcester, and Herend. The logo also appeared on a wide range of merchandise available at the Royal Tournament Shop.

The Australian Tri-Service Massed Bands made the trip to London in 1987, in advance of the bicentenary year of the founding of Australia in 1988. The Royal Engineers were also celebrating their 200th Anniversary in 1987, in a display entitled RE200, members of the Corps constructed a series of life-size objects in darkness in the arena using poles covered in ultraviolet paint which were only visible when the UV light was switched on. This included a bridge, which was then 'demolished' by another team of Engineers. Although UV effects are common now, they were at the forefront of theatrical technology in the mid-1980s, and nobody was using the effect on the same scale as the Tournament.

An even more complicated backcloth followed in 1888, "The Year of the Drum", it was covered with a series of massive 3D Drums, many had platforms big enough to accommodate groups of drummers for the opening (one had a full Drum Kit, played by an RAF musician). The four drums, spanning the width of the arena, could be lifted on hoists to allow performers to enter and exit the arena. There were also large drums pulled into place on the Royal Box and Non-Royal Box entrances at the Warwick Road end of the arena, for the opening of the show, Chinese Drummers were placed on to top of one and Native American Drummers on the other.

There was much talk at the time about the centrepiece for the 1988 Tournament, a circular lighting truss was lowered in the centre of the arena with a revolving platform in the middle. It was pre-set on the arena floor before the opening began, being raised 80 ft as this section of the show drew to a close. As the rig was lifted, the fabric tube unfurled to create a

40 - Design of the 1988 Backcloth by Maj Micheal Parker

huge replica of Sir Francis Drake's Drum. This was impressive enough, but Maj Parker wanted to add three drummers and a Standard Bearer to the revolving platform to be raised 80 ft on the drum. The safety of the performers was a key consideration, it was decided that it was better to teach some Aerial Erectors from the RAF how to drum, rather than elevate some professional drummers. This worked perfectly and created one of the most dramatic moments of any Royal Tournament.

Francis Drake's Drum also appeared in the finale (minus the drummers who had climbed up ladders into the roof following their cameo). 1988 marked the 300th anniversary of the defeat of the Spanish Armada. Models of Spanish and British Ships were specially created for the finale, mounted on Army issue Land Rover's. The ships were fitted with pyro, which was fired as they engaged in battle, they could also roll with the waves as the inevitable British weather played its part in the battle. Soldiers dressed in 16th Century Uniforms, carrying smaller 'fire boats' above their heads, marched out to meet the Spanish ships in the arena, causing the Armada to flee the scene, leaving Drake's Navy triumphant.

In the late 1980s the Royal Tournament funded a project for new compositions of music which would entertain audiences and be enjoyable for performers. Under the guiding influence. of Commissioning Editor Lt. Col. Frank Renton, who was Director of Music at Kneller Hall at the time the Royal Tournament Series was born. One of the commissions was Royal Tournament, Op 115 by Derek Bourgeois.

Changes at Earls Court impacted greatly on the 1989 Tournament. The Chair Store, located behind the arena doors held the ground floor seating blocks when the building was setup for exhibitions such as the Ideal Home Show. For the duration of the Tournament each summer, it had provided the perfect space for the temporary stables for the King's Troop Royal Horse Artillery and any other equine displays. Earls Court Two, a vast hanger-like exhibition hall was now under construction, increasing the exhibition space by 17,000 m^2. The Chair Store was demolished in order to create a new link bridge over the railway line which divided the two buildings.

The building works meant that it was not possible to have the usual central set of arena doors in the backcloth. This was overcome by adding curtained entrances set at angles on each side of the backcloth, allowing the King's Troop for example to form up on K Ramp (outside the building) and walk into the arena for their display – a rather slower entrance and exit for the Musical Drive than usual.

The backdrop itself was constructed from blue fabric; a huge RAF Crest suspended over a set of white steps which were large enough for the entire Massed Bands to form up on before their performance. The Eagle on the RAF Crest had a 70ft wingspan, it was suspended from a track and could be 'flown' down to the centre of the arena for the finale sequence. Historic Aircraft were wheeled into the arena in front of the curtained entrances, during the Massed Bands Display. Two projection screens were also concealed behind the blue fabric, they were revealed to show the intro film before the Field Gun Competition. A huge set of blue fabric curtains could be pulled across the entire backcloth to enable scene changes on the white steps.

The theme of the 1989 show was "The History of Flight", a real owl flew the length of the arena to open each performance, followed by a life-size model of Leonardo da Vinci's Flying Machine (made by Mervyn

Harridence) which was flown (with the help of some rigging) down the arena as well. The show also marked the 40th anniversary of NATO with representatives all the member countries.

ELEVEN – PUSHING BOUNDARIES

The show continued to evolve technically as it entered the next decade. 1990 marked the 100th Year that the Tournament had been performed (10 had been missed due to the First and Second World Wars). This was a Royal Navy year, and the theme was "The History of the Royal Marines", it told the story from 28 October 1664, when the Duke of York and Albany's Maritime Regiment of Foot was formed.

The backcloth included side wings covered by a helicopter, aircraft carrier, and white Ensign. Two huge red curtains with golden anchors could be opened to show the side of H.M.S. Victory, complete with 1805 Marines on the deck, firing muskets during the opening of the show (they were actually suspended on harnesses, raised into position by hoists).

41 - Royal Marines arctic scene and ski slope 1990

The backcloth was transformed for the Royal Marines battle, the curtains opening further to allow the side of Victory to be lowered down to the arena floor revealing an arctic scene, complete with ski slope and ski jump. The dramatic transformation took place to atmospheric music before the Marines made their assault of the snowy cliff. Once their objective had been met, they then extracted via the ski slope and 'death slides,' the more accomplished RM skiers taking on the ski jump enroute back to the arena floor.

Unfortunately, this display had to be cancelled for a few performances in the middle of the Tournament run. This was due to the lower section of the ski slope breaking under the weight of the 100-stong Royal Marine Display Team who had formed up on the slope for a souvenir photo – it took a few days to remove and replace the collapsed panels.

For the finale, the Massed Bands of HM Royal Marines, under the direction of Lieutenant Colonel J. M. Ware (Principal Director of Music) were joined by the Band & Drill Team of the Spanish Marine Corps, United States Marine Corps 2nd Marine Division Band, and the Royal Netherlands Marine Corps as well as the King's Squad, Royal Marines. During the finale, a 60 ft high representation of The Royal Marines Cap Badge was due to be lowered from the roof above the assembled cast. The Cap Badge includes the Battle Honour of "Gibraltar," the Spanish Marine Corps were not pleased by this. Maj. Parker came up with a solution (avoiding a potential political problem), the battle honour was removed, creating The Royal Marines Collar Badge Which doesn't include the Battle Honour. The finale also included Sunset and the Naval Prayer, read by HRH The Duke of Edinburgh, Captain General, Royal Marines.

The following year (1991) was themed "The Year of the Horse" with the Army in the lead, displays included "A Royal Joust" by the Knights of Arkley (although due to a sponsorship tie-in with a well know window company, they were listed as "The Anglian Knights" in the programme), The Mounted Band of the Blues & Royals and Household Cavalry, Musical Drive by the King's Troop, Royal Horse Artillery and a recreation of the Charge of the Light Brigade at the Battle of Balaclava. There was also a demonstration of modern Armoured Reconnaissance (with vehicles which had recently returned from the Gulf following the end of hostilities a few months earlier) and Historical Armoured Cars, both displays showing the evolution of Cavalry from Horse to Armoured Vehicle. The Massed Bands were drawn from across the Cavalry Regiments and Royal Tank Regiment. The Finale was a "Salute to the Horse" and featured representatives from Mounted Cavalry from around the World.

The backcloth design once again created challenges for Mervyn Harridence (painter of the huge artworks) and Unusual Rigging (responsible for hanging them and making them move). The design included large representations of Cavalry Headdress (Busbie's, Cavalry Helmet's, and

Shako's) across the ages. Six 3-D headdress were suspended from the lighting rig and could be hidden behind the Proscenium Arch or lowered to the floor in front of the arena doors, behind there were huge representations of Household Cavalry State Trumpets and Banners, Hussars Jackets, and a Sabretache[27], all of which were suspended from tracks and could be hidden behind the wings or flown into position.

42 - Maj Micheal Parker and Mervyn Harridence discussing the details for the headdress for the 1991 Backcloth, a finished 3rd Dragoons Trooper Helmet in the background

The Inter-Services Dismounted Skill-at-Arms competition returned to the Tournament in 1991. It had taken place elsewhere for the previous three years due to the ongoing re-development of Earls Court. The competition included Foil, Épée, and Sabre.

"Heroes of the Air" was the theme for the RAF in 1992. The show started with the Creation of the World, moved on to Man's First Flight, and finished by going "Into Space" in the finale. The Queen's Colour Squadron performed with the Massed Bands of the Royal Air Force. The ever-popular RAF Police Dogs also appeared, and the RAF Regiment provided an exciting action display.

The backcloth was made up of 60 ft high Periaktos (3-sided rotating columns), one face was painted with an RAF Harrier aircraft, a second was white and acted as a super-size projection screen, and the third was covered in acrylic mirrors reflecting the performers back to the audience. During the Massed Bands Display at the end of the first half of the show, a revolving platform with a full-size grand piano was lowered from the ceiling in the centre of the arena, the pianist, Flt Lt Stuart Stirling played 'Rhapsody in Blue'.

---

[27] A cavalry bag or pouch, worn suspended from the belt of a soldier along with his sabre

The Royal Military Police 'The Redcaps' display in 1992 brought together mounted police and riders on motorbikes. In the first part of the display, the team performed a musical ride with six horses and six motorbikes including tight crossovers and jumping brush fences. In the second half of the display, the horse riders and motorcyclists competed in a tent pegging competition.

Wimbledon based PR Company; Kestrel Communications were appointed to manage the Public Relations for the Tournament in 1992. The account was managed by Janine Hood (now Hislop) before permanently moving over to the Royal Tournament staff in 1995. In later years, Janine was assisted by Harriet Jarman (now Nelson) and supported at Earls Court during the show weeks by Lynne Price (now Parsons) and Katherine Browne.

The theme for the Navy year in 1993 was "Victory at Sea". For the opening, the centre of the backcloth was a map of the Atlantic, with the Americas on the left and Europe and North Africa on the right, and a White Ensign either side on the wings with famous Naval Battle Honours listed. The base of the backcloth was painted with white-capped waves. The centre of the map divided and opened to reveal the bow of H.M.S. Victory. A vast Royal Marines Corps of Drums and Massed Bands entered from the wave covered arena doors in smoke and under dramatic lighting.

43 - Design of the 1993 Backcloth by Maj Micheal Parker

The Royal Army Veterinary Corps provided a Dog Display Team in 1993. The volunteer dog handlers had trained in their own time for the display, which included a range of service dog demonstrations such as protection dogs and search capabilities.

The 1993 programme also included a Band from the Russian Navy, complete with dancers. Another spectacular Trafalgar Finale followed. The map on the backcloth opened up further to reveal French and British ships on either side of the Victory model (which was now showing "England expects that every man will do his duty" in semaphore flags). The two fleets were suspended from tracks on the lighting rig and were now drawn out on either side of the arena above the white pith helmets of the Massed Bands before the ships engaged in a pyrotechnic battle. The Royal Navy Display Team once again gave a mast manning display as part of the finale sequence.

The duration of the Tournament was reduced in 1993 from 18 days to 12, the number of performances was now 22 (from 30). Col. Ferguson had addressed the issue in his foreword to the programme the previous year saying that the Ministry of Defence had reviewed the length of the Tournament due to reductions in the strength of all three Armed Services. For the first time in its history a Sunday Matinee was added in to the to the run.

The theme for 1994 was "A Force for Good", the backcloth included the 16 flags of NATO with the Globe and Laurel of the United Nations Emblem in the middle. The opening, "Armageddon" included 12 ft high representations of the Four Horsemen of the Apocalypse (Conquest, Slaughter, Famine, and Death), which were repelled by the Massed Corps of Drums of the NATO Countries (a symbol of Good over Evil).

For the Royal Engineers in Action display, six Hydrema earth moving vehicles were put through their paces in the arena in a modern twist on the Musical Drive. The vehicles were then used to create an Ark, an interpretation of Noah's biblical boat in the arena. There followed a parade of animals who had served with the Armed Forces, from elephants and camels to horses and dogs, as well as mascots including a Shetland Pony, goat, a python, and even a tarantula (which legend has it, escaped at Earls Court and was replaced from a local pet shop).

Competition had been at the heart of the Tournament since its inception, and the Ark was transformed to ARRC. In 1994, Troops from the NATO Allied Rapid Reaction Corps (ARRC), competed over a challenging assault course in the arena under the direction of Lt Col Richard Quicke, Light Dragoons and WO1 Mike Bell, RAF (an ex-Portsmouth B Crew Field Gunner).

The Massed Bands and Bugles of The Light Division made their last appearance at the Royal Tournament in 1994. The Bandsmen came from the four regimental bands; Corunna, Salamanca, Normandy, and Peninsula with Buglers from both the Light Division and The Royal Green Jackets. They were joined with the Band and Massed Pipes & Drums of The Royal Gurkha Rifles. The performance included 'High on a Hill', 'Keel Row', 'Road to the Isle', and finished with 'Zorba the Greek' which started at a slow march and finished at Rifle Pace (140 paces per minute).

1995 marked the 50th Anniversary of the end of the Second World War, the theme was "Victory 50 years on". The backcloth was dominated by a red letter 'V' in the centre, St Paul's Cathedral was depicted behind it with the RAF moto "Per Ardua ad Astra" (Through Adversity to the Stars) arched over it. The years of the war, 1939 and 1945 were also painted in red on the wings. Either side of the central section, two London streets were painted, one intact (as at the start of the war) and one 'bombed out' after the Bitz.

This was another international Tournament with music from the US Army Band Europe, The Central Band of The Russian Federation, The Band of the French Foreign Legion, The Canadian Forces' Air Command Band, and The Royal Australian Air Force Central Band as well as the Massed Bands of the Royal Air Force under the Direction of Wing Commander R.E. Wilkinson.

The Finale included a Victory parade with music from the RAF Squadronaires playing 'In the Mood' (Miller) and the massed bands (with audience participation) played songs from the Second World War era; 'Bless 'am All' (Stillman/Lake/Hughes), and 'Land of Hope and Glory' (Elgar). Following the 1995 Royal Tournament, £100,000 was donated to Armed Forces Charities.

For the Royal Navy lead year in 1996, the theme was "Rule Britannia". The impressive backcloth including crashing, white-capped waves extending from the wings across the arena doors. A pair of Royal Navy Submariner Dolphins were painted across the arena doors. These 12 ft long sea creatures were painted by hand, in situ, by Mervyn Harridence while the rehearsals were going on around him.

Two projectors were mounted within the backcloth projecting images from naval history onto water screens, created by thousands of litres of water being pumped to the height of the backcloth and cascading down to form the screen. There were also a set of 'dancing fountains' incorporated into the design which were timed to move with the music of the Massed

Bands. During the opening sequence, British Actor Garard Green read an excerpt from William Shakespeare's Richard II, ending with the line "This blessed plot, this earth, this realm, this England" as the Massed Bands of HM Royal Marines entered the arena.

The ships crest of H.M.S. Sovereign was suspended in front of a set of blue curtains which opened to reveal a cliff face for the Royal Marines to assault once more. Following their successful battle, they extracted to the sea as an inflatable submarine extended into the arena with lasers on the balcony level giving the impression that it was partially submerged. Raiding craft and frogmen suspended from the ceiling on wires helped to create the underwater illusion.

44 - An early design of the 1996 Backcloth by Maj Micheal Parker. This version included the North Atlantic map from the 1993 Backcloth, it was replaced with blue curtains behind the H.M.S. Sovereign crest in the final version.

The Royal Naval Display Team performed a window ladder display and a display of Physical Training which included a traditional Hornpipe, and modern aerobics display to a recording of "Ooh Aah... Just a Little Bit" by Gina G (The UK Entry to the Eurovision Song Contest earlier in the year, finishing 8th). Audience members were invited into the arena at the end of the display to have a go themselves, this was compered by Jet, Rhino, or Cobra from The Gladiators television series.

Irish Dancing had also been brought back into the public eye by the Riverdance performance at the Eurovision Song Contest in 1994. An Irish Traditional Youth Band and Dancers from Dublin and Cork travelled to London to take part in "The Emerald Isle" display at the 1996 Tournament, the performers were aged between 8 and 21. They performed alongside the Pipes & Drums of the Queen's Royal Hussars and the Irish Guards as well as the Band, Pipes, Drums, and Bugles of the Royal Irish Regiment, and the Band of the Royal Ulster Constabulary.

A new Official Photographer was appointed in 1996, Sam Lloyd and his team went on to photograph the Royal Tournament up until the Last Run. Going on to be the Official Photographer for the Royal Military Tattoo 2000 and later the British Military Tournament. Sam has uploaded his archive of images from the 1996 – 1999 Tournaments to his website www.tournamentimages.com. The service photographer at this time was Sgt Ian Liptrott, Grenadier Guards.

45 - Royal Navy Field Gun Competition 1996

The dates for the 1996 Tournament were earlier than usual, the show opened on 9 July and closed on 20 July with a view to avoiding a clash with television coverage of the Summer Olympics in Atlanta (USA) from July 19 to August 4. Rather than one week of the run being during the school term and the second being in the summer holidays, both weeks in 1996 were during the school holidays. The move severely impacted ticket sales, for performances during the first week the top floor of Earls Court, affectionately known as 'The God's', was closed with ticket holders re-seated in the stalls or balcony seats.

The King's Troop Royal Horse Artillery celebrated their 50th Anniversary in 1997 and their badge was the central feature of the backcloth for that year. The backcloth was painted by theatre scenery company Victor Mara Ltd in 1997.

The theme was Firepower and traced the history of artillery, the opening included champion archers from the Army firing flaming arrows at targets in front of the arena doors. There was also a pageant of Artillery Through the Ages and a display showing the "Modern Gunner" by 19 Regiment illustrating how Air Mobile Guns could be brought into action. The Massed Bands of the Household Division and Mounted Band of The Blues & Royals (RHG/D) performance included an arrangement called "Hint of Spice", arranged by Bandmaster David Millgate it incorporated a selection of hits from the Spice Girls (just a year after their debut single, "Wannabe" was released).

46 - The Massed Bands of the Household Division and Mounted Band of The Blues & Royals (RHG/D) performing "Hint of Spice"

The New Zealand Defence Force Māori Culture Group brought 70 serving members of the New Zealand Armed Forces to take part in the 1997 Tournament. The group performed Waiata (songs) and a Haka in the arena. They were also persuaded to perform the Haka outside the Field Gun Bar's after the show one evening, much to the delight of the assembled audience of performers, crew, and Tournament staff.

The Flying Gunners, the motorcycle display team of the Royal Artillery, also performed at the '97 Tournament. The finale of the show was "1812", with

Guns from the King's Troop, RHA, Trumpeters from the Mounted Band of the Blues & Royals (RHG/D), and the Massed Bands of the Household Division under the Direction of Lt. Col. D.E. Price, Senior Director of Music.

1997 also marked a switch in the television coverage for the Tournament, the move was made from the BBC to ITV with Phillip Schofield as the presenter. In addition, the Gladiators returned to the Tournament in 1997, this time, taking on 'volunteers' from the Royal Navy, Army, and Royal Air Force in "The Duel" from their popular ITV programme.

There was also a change of Chairman in 1997, Major-General Sir Iain Mackay-Dick who had served as Major-General Commanding the Household Division & General Officer Commanding London District handed over to Major-General Sir Evelyn Webb-Carter. The tradition of the GOC London District also taking on the role of Chairman of the Tournament had gone back over a century to the appointment of Major-General Lord Methuen in 1896.

Micheal Parker had been unwell during the mid-1990s, as Producer, he had led the creative direction of the Tournament for over 20 years. The decision was taken to install an Assistant Producer for the first time before the 1997 Tournament who would be able to stand in as Producer if required. Major (later Major General) Simon Brooks-Ward of the Royal Yeomanry was appointed to the role.

The Royal Air Force took the lead in 1998 with the theme "The Story of Flight". The show opened with a with a huge replica volcano in the centre of the arena, as it erupted, an inflatable globe emerged to symbolise the creation of the Earth and the beginning of time. A real Eagle Owl flew dramatically down length of the darkened arena under a spotlight followed by the return of the Da Vinci flying machine doing the same.

The Massed Bands of the Royal Air Force provided the soundtrack for the opening under the direction of Wing Commander R.K. Wiffin, this included the futuristic theme from Star Trek 'Deep Space Nine' (Goldsmith). The baton was handed to Squadron Leader Mark Luton, who directed the Massed Bands and Pipes as they were joined by the Queen's Colour Squadron.

The Band of the South Australian Police performed a specially arranged programme of Australian and British favourites, they were joined by the energetic Australian All-Star Dance Team for their performance. The audience were also treated to a trick riding display by Cossacks from the recently independent Ukraine[28]. The riders and their horses had been transported by the Ukrainian Air Force using an adapted Ilyushin Il-76 aircraft.

The 1998 finale was "Into the Future", the Massed Bands and Pipers returned to the tune of "Summon the Heroes" by John Williams before taking a tour around the universe with extracts form The Planets by Gustav Holst. In place of a painted backcloth in 1998, vast amounts of Starcloth were suspended across the end of the arena and above the lighting truss, covered with thousands of white LED lights. Hidden above the lighting rig, behind the starcloth were five aircraft and a full set of inflatable planets which could all be lowered into view on cue. Torches were also issued to the audience so that they could become stars themselves in the finale. The finale music included 'Highland Cathedral' (Korb), and 'Holyrood; (Alford)and the poem "High Flight" (an airman's ecstasy) by John Gillespie Magee.

An unusual RAF Action act was given by 34 Squadron, RAF Regiment. Breaking away from the now traditional airfield defence display, 34 Squadron brought motorbikes and Land Rover's into the arena, choreographed to 'It's Like That', debut single of American hip hop group Run-D.M.C which had been remixed by House Music DJ Jason Nevins in 1997. Members of the Squadron also abseiled and parachuted into the arena, to great applause from the audience. To end the display, all the members of 34 Regiment clustered into the centre of the arena and were encircled by the Queen's Colour Squadron, as a pyrotechnic was set off, the members of 34 Regiment removed their desert combat jackets and the covers from their helmets to reveal coloured t-shirts and painted helmets to create an inner circle of red, a white outer circle, and the blue of the Queen's Colour Squadron to create a human version of the RAF Roundel. Another example of the Royal Tournament reinventing itself and trying new things to engage with new audiences.

* * *

The modern twist on the RAF Action act had proved to be popular with the audience at Earls Court, it had also impressed the other performers in the

---

[28] Became independent from the Soviet Union with the Act of Declaration of Independence of Ukraine, 24 August 1991.

show. A 'special performance' was staged in the Portsmouth Field Gun Bar late one evening. The three temporary Field Gun Bars were built in the Philbeach Hall on the balcony level of Earls Court each year and were a hub for the performers to unwind each evening, The roof of the hall was 70 ft heigh. On this particular evening, the music switched to 'It's Like That' and a pyro charge went off high above the bar in a "fire bucket" filled with red, white, and blue confetti which rained down on the assembled group below as they were ushered to the sides of the bar creating a 'safe space' in the middle. Abseil bags were dropped from the ceiling and waves of 34 Regiment descended to the bar level. They were greeted with drinks from the bar staff and huge rounds of applause.

The Tournament had a unique social life of its own. Illustrations from the Islington Days showed members of the various regiments taking part, enjoying a drink together in the makeshift accommodation in the gallery of the Agricultural Hall. The majority of the cast of the Tournament were usually accommodated in the building (Agricultural Hall, Olympia, and Earls Court) with a few exceptions in the latter years; Officers were accommodated in local hotels, some overseas performers were put up in transit accommodation around London, and London based performers would travel back to their home accommodation each evening. Those who 'lived in', away from their usual barracks, ships, establishments etc. would often head out into the local area and were generally welcomed by the Landlords of Islington and later Kensington and Earls Court.

There are anecdotal stories of the pubs around Earls Court being used as unofficial Messes for the various acts taking part, providing a space to relax between performances. As "The Troubles" in Northern Ireland escalated, the threat of attacks on the mainland grew, it was decided that the potential soft target of servicemen in the pubs around Earls Court needed to be addressed. Rules were drawn up and issued to visiting units each year on where they were allowed to go for a drink and wearing uniform in public was now not encouraged.

Officers and Senior NCO's working on the Tournament had their own respective Messes where they took their meals each day. As is traditional in the Armed Forces, bars were opened in these Messes each evening. Meals for other ranks were served in Mr Green's Restaurant in the basement of Earls Court, a purpose-built space which could accommodate the hundreds of performers who were fed three times a day for the duration of the Tournament by Armed Forces chefs.

Next to Mr Green's was a fully equipped pub which was run as a 'Junior Ranks Club' by the Support Unit who were assigned to the Royal Tournament each year. They also provided the Arena Party, QM facility, and administration of the backstage running of the show.

In addition to the Officer's, SNCO's, and Junior Ranks Messes, three 'Pop-up Bar's' were installed at Earls Court. Built from 'wooden flats' used for temporary exhibition stands, the walls of the bars were dressed in the colours of the respective Field Gun Crews, Blue of Portsmouth, Red for Devonport, and Green for Fleet Air Arm.

The Field Gun Bars became legendary. Managed by staff from the three Field Gun Crew's, they provided a space for performers to relax and socialise without leaving the building (most were accommodated on site or in local hotels for Senior Staff), the public were also welcome providing a unique opportunity to meet some of the performers from the show. The evening performances didn't finish until 2230 hrs, the bars were open until 'late' often with entertainment – as mentioned earlier these regularly involved performers from the show.

The last week of the Tournament each year included a series of parties. The 'Arena Party' was open to everyone as a thank you for their efforts in making the show a success. A DJ was usually engaged for the party, plugging into the vast arena sound and light system creating arguably the biggest night club in London. A barbeque and bar were set up in the arena for the 2,000 participants. However, the public the following day would never have known, as the arena was returned to its normal pristine state long before the doors opened.

More exclusive 'ticket only' parties also took place on the evenings earlier in the last week. The Police Party was staged in the SNCO's Mess and tickets were highly sought after. The Ushers Party was staged in various locations over the years, behind the backcloth on the balcony level or in one of the non-used halls at Earls Court. Hundreds of serving personnel from all three services would volunteer each year as Military Ushers, a tradition dating back to 1882, when the show was brought "Entirely under Military Management". These Ushers worked in shifts across the duration of the Tournament, engaging with the thousands of visitors each day, bridging the gap between the public and the Armed Forces – regularly being asked to pose for photos with groups of visitors who wanted to show that they had met a serviceman or servicewoman at the show.

47 - The Last Run Programme cover 1999

TWELVE – THE LAST RUN

In his forward to the programme for the 1998 Royal Tournament, Col. Iain Ferguson had hinted about the future of the show. He mentioned that "today's Armed Forces are finely tuned and trimmed to match the roles they perform in the defence of our country. There is no fat. This makes it ever harder to stage the Royal Tournament – the largest military tattoo in the world."

The newly elected Labour Government began its Strategic Defence Review (SDR) in May 1997, an SDR White Paper was published on 8 July 1998. Col. Iain remarked that "The Ministry of Defence are considering the future of the Royal Tournament" but there would be "no changes until 1999". However, in his look ahead to the following year he mentioned that the "Massed Bands of the Royal Marines, the Household Division, and the Royal Air Force" would be taking part in 1999 – the first time that a tri-service Massed Bands had been assembled since the Centenary Show in 1980.

On 14 September 1998, the Ministry of Defence announced that the 1999 Royal Tournament would be the last. The BBC reported that that Defence Secretary George Robertson said: "The Royal Tournament has served us well for a great many years, but as we approach the millennium, it is timely for us to take a fresh look at this traditional event." He went on to say that "This is a new beginning, not an end of the Tournament, and my aim is to make it more relevant and modern, whilst retaining an element of pageantry."

Planning had already begun for the 1999 show which was given the subtitle 'The Last Run'. The aim was for the show to go out with a Bang and not a whimper. The Tournament opened on Tuesday 20 July. The programme included many of the displays which had been established at the Tournament since 1880. An additional show was added to the usual run, on Monday 2 August, so that the last show would be an evening performance rather than the Sunday matinee.

Colonel Iain Ferguson wrote a history of the Tournament which was included in the souvenir programme of the 1999 Royal Tournament. This history brought together the work of Lt. Col. Binns and Lord Chalfont, summarising the 120-year history of the show.

Catie Bland, who had been Personal Assistant to Maj Micheal Parker for many years moved across to support the Royal Tournament office as event

Administrator to support the delivery of the Last Run. Catie went on to be involved in the RMT2000 and QM100 in the following year. Emma Bagwell Purefoy (Later Parker) had worked on many of Micheal Parker's events during the 1990s, she took on the role of PA to Maj Parker for the 1999 Tournament.

The backcloth for 1999 included the Royal Cypher of the Sovereign; Queen Victoria, who originally gave the 'Royal' prefix, Edward VII, George V, Edward VIII, and George VI. The cypher of Queen Elizabeth II was painted onto a gauze in the centre of the backcloth with Her Majesty's Royal Standard behind. A Garter Arch was also included, surrounded by flags on each side: a White Ensign, an Army Standard, and an RAF Colour as well as a Union Flag. A ribbon at the top of the design read "The Last Royal Tournament" with the years 1880 and 1999 at either end. A second ribbon was painted across the front of the platform where the arena doors were mounted with another Royal Motto: 'Dieu et mon droit' ('God and my right'). The plant badges of the United Kingdom - rose, thistle and shamrock – were also included.

48 - Design of the final Royal Tournament Backcloth by Maj Micheal Parker

The last Royal Tournament backcloth was painted by Graham Menage. It was rigged by Alan Jacobi's Unusual Rigging Ltd. The company were involved in the technical side of the Tournament for 18 years and were listed as the show riggers from 1987 (taking over from Barrett Brothers).

The Opening of the show was a pageant of "The Royal Tournament 1880-1999", music was provided by the Tri Service Massed Bands under the direction of Lieutenant Colonel P.E. Hills, Grenadier Guards. All of the performers paraded through the centre the arena in order of their first appearance in the Tournament timeline, returning on the sides of the arena, through doors in the backcloth to the holding area in Earls Court 2. The first to enter the arena were two cavalry troopers at the gallop, each cutting through two "heads and posts", linking back to one of the most popular displays of the Grand Military Tournament and Assault-at-Arms.

49 - Opening of the Royal Tournament 1999, Entrance of the King's Troop Royal Horse Artillery

At each performance, two gun-teams from the King's Troop, Royal Horse Artillery took part in this pageant, with the exception of the performance for HM Queen Elizabeth and for the Princess Royal. On these two nights, the entire King's Troop took part in the pageant, six gun-teams with outriders and a full complement of mounted officers. Additional carpet was laid (to protect the floor) for these performances, from the Warwick Road entrances of the arena to the outside of Earls Court, enabling the guns to be pulled through the arena and then taken outside to return to the backstage area.

The Musical Ride was performed by the Household Cavalry, acknowledging the first 'display' to be performed at the Tournament in 1882. This was followed by the Musical Drive by the King's Troop, Royal Horse Artillery, over a century after the first Musical Drive was performed by D Battery Royal Horse Artillery in 1896.

The Royal Signals Motorcycle Display Team (The White Helmets) also performed, marking the fact that the first Motorcycle Display by Despatch

Riders of the Training Battalion, Royal Corps of Signals was staged at Olympia in 1931. Another audience favourite to appear at the Last Run was the Royal Air Force Police Dog Display Team, RAF Police Dogs had first appeared half a century earlier at the 1949 Tournament. The display team was disbanded in 1994 but was reformed for the 1999 Tournament.

The first half of the show was brought to a close by the spectacular Tri-Service Massed Bands under the direction of Lieutenant Colonel Richard Waterer, Principal Director of Music, Royal Marines. The music included: 'Aces High' (Goodwin), 'The Olympic Spirit' (Williams), 'Star Trek Generations' (McCarthy), and a new composition by Lt. Col. Waterer 'Royal Salute'. The Massed Bands were joined by the Tri-Service Choir under the Direction of Captain S. Barnwell, Clive Band, Prince of Wales Division.

In it's now established position, after the interval, the Royal Navy Field Gun Competition opened the second half of each performance. Since the first run at Olympia in 1907, Field Gun had been a huge audience favourite. Generations of spectators had applauded the elite athletes of the Royal Navy, stepping out into the arena in their 'white fronts' to the tune of 'Heart of Oak' (Boyce). Then cheering them through the Run Out, Run Back, and Run Home. On Friday 29 July 1999 the Devonport Field Gun Crew set a new record of 2 mins 40.43 secs just days before the final performance. Breaking a record set by Portsmouth in 1984.

In the presence of HRH The Princess Royal on the evening of Monday 2 August 1999, the last Field Gun Competition was staged, the competing crews were Portsmouth and Fleet Air Arm, although every Field Gunner from every crew (both A and B Crews) were in the arena that night along with their support staff. The four corners of the arena were full of white fronts as well.

It has been well documented that the Field Gunners and support staff wore black arm bands during the final run (although they had been told not to). At the end of the run, when they two competing crews would usually form up between the ramps on the Royal Box Side of the arena, hundreds of Field Gunners poured into the space, as the audience gave a standing ovation in recognition of the efforts of every Field Gunner who had ever competed.

In his closing announcement following the lynch out, commentator Basil Reitz said "The Last Run. And so, a formidable, and what we have described over the years as the toughest team competition in the world, marches into history." The 12,500-sellout crowd at Earls Court, roared their disapproval that they had witnessed the Last Field Gun Competition at the Tournament.

There were no black arm bands however, when the crews returned to the arena later in the show for the presentation of the trophies. The crews were now wearing their coloured crew jackets. The presentations were made by HRH The Princess Royal:

- Inter-Command Challenge Cup - Devonport
- Aggregate Time Cup - Devonport
- Fastest Time Cup - Devonport
- Least Penalty Points – Fleet Air Arm
- Copenhagen Cup – Fleet Air Arm

Silver medals were awarded to the members of the Devonport Crew, and Bronze Medals were awarded to Portsmouth and Fleet Air Arm.

* * *

The following section of the programme was the "Mounted Competitions, Special Events, & Tug of War". This section of the show changed from performance to performance but was most closely linked to the original Tournament in 1880, it included Tug of War and Mounted Skill-At-Arms.

The Tug of War competition in 1999 was staged during the evening performances of first week, with a different weight category each day. The teams would 'weigh-in' first thing each morning before the preliminary rounds took place, the four best teams for the day would then be seeded for the competition in the arena that evening. Three ropes were set out by the admin party: one on the Royal Box Side and one on the Non-Royal Box Side. The winners of the best of three 'pulls' on each rope would go through to the final, on the third rope, placed in the centre of the arena directly in front of the Royal Box. The marker used in for the final pulls was a 2m long Hippocamp (symbol of the Royal Tournament), for the Last Run in 1999 tears were added to its eye.

The competition had changed little in the 120 years of the Tournament but was still popular with the audience, who cheered on their favourite team (or the one closest to them) at each performance. The Tug of War Competition was coordinated by Major J. Grimes, Royal Artillery and Captain C. Sayer, Royal Yeomanry. The Royal Yeomanry also provided support staff for the duration of the competition each year.

50 - Tug of War c. 1887 - Royal Military Tournament Booklet

The Mounted Skill-At-Arms took place under the direction of Col. Alec Jackson towards the end of the second week - Tent Pegging at both performances on Thursday 29 July and Sword, Lance, & Revolver at the Matinee on Friday 30 July. The individual Tent Pegging had changed little since the Islington days. Two competitors would enter the arena from the Warwick Road end at a canter, lower their lances to 'attack' their tent peg at the gallop, marks were awarded for picking up and carrying the peg over the carry line. They then swapped sides and repeated the exercise.

In the team Tent Pegging competition, teams of three from each participating unit took part. Each team galloped twice down the arena 'line abreast' each member attacking their own peg. Lances were used on the first run; swords were used on the second. Marks were awarded for striking or carrying the peg as well as "for style as a team."

The early mounted competitions of the 1880s had evolved over time. Heads and Posts (noted in the programme as a "decapitating sweep") and lemon cutting (noted as a vertical downward cut) gave way in to Dummy Thrusting in 1911, this continued until 1939. In 1914, the pistol was added to Tent Pegging and Dummy Thrusting to become "Sword, Lance, and Revolver" which continued until the last Tournament in 1999.

Each competitor for Sword, Lance, and Revolver would ride the course on their own, crossing the start line at a canter, they would jump the first fence with the sword 'sloped' against their shoulder. As the horse accelerated, the sword was brought down to engage and thrust at the first dummy (on the offside). They slowed down to take the second fence before accelerating to thrust at the second dummy (on the nearside), the sward would remain in this dummy and the rider would draw their revolver from its holster. They then fired (a blank) at a ballon on the right of a fence as they jumped it, then at a second on the ground, and a third on the right of another fence before re-holstering the revolver while at a canter. The rider would then collect a lance from a stand and accelerating to a gallop, lowering the lance and attacking a tent peg. The rider had 45 seconds to complete the course.

The Royal Tournament Show Jumping competitions also stemmed from the Grand Military Tournament days. Team Show Jumping began as the Section Jumping competition in 1887. The Officers' Jumping competition started in 1891, His Majesty King George V presented his cup for this competition in 1913 which then became known as the King's Cup. From 1947 the King's Cup was open to all ranks.

The competitions were staged under British Show Jumping Association Rules, with the various cups being competed for at the Tournament:

- Princess Anne's Cup (Newcomers Standard)
- Prince of Wales' Cup (Newcomers Regional Final Standard)
- King's Cup (Foxhunter Standard)
- Team Jumping (Novice Standard)
- Queen's Cup (top 6 Prince of Wales Cup and top 6 King's Cup)

Another equestrian special event in 1999 was the Metropolitan Police Activity Ride, a display which brought together operational mounted officers to demonstrate their expert riding skills. While negotiating a series of brush fences in the arena, the riders removed and replaced their tunics, stirrup irons and finally saddles while the horses continued to jump.

Other special events in 1999 included: presentation of the Services Sports Awards, Sea Cadets, RNLI 175 Anniversary, Massed Royal Naval Volunteer Bands, Portsmouth Area Volunteer Cadet Corps Field Gun Competition, Royal Air Force Association, St John Ambulance, Corps of Drums Society, Massed Bands of the Royal Marines Cadets, Royal British Legion, and Royal Naval Association.

On the evening of 26 July, the night that Her Majesty the Queen attended, the special event was a "Parade of Field Gunners". It was estimated that 15,000 Field Gunners had taken part in the competition since its inception in 1907. This one-off tribute to the generations of Field Gunners included Sea Cadets, the 1999 Field Gun Crews, and ex-field gunners from Portsmouth, Devonport, Fleet Air Arm, and Chatham. This group included the oldest living field gunner at the time, 99-year-old Bill Bedford, who had run for Portsmouth at the 1923 Royal Tournament at Olympia. The original ship's bell from H.M.S. Terrible, one of the two ships which landed the men and guns in South Africa, was brought into the arena and was rung to "end the watch".

* * *

The first Massed Pipes & Drums appeared at the Royal Naval and Military Tournament in 1911, for the final year the Massed Pipes & Drums included bands from across the Commonwealth; The Royal Australian Regiment, The Cameron Highlanders of Ottawa (Canada), New Zealand Police, Transvaal Scottish Regiment (South Africa), Queen's Own Hussars, London Irish Rifles, 101st (Northumbrian) Regiment, and 40 Regiment Royal Artillery. The Australian State Coach was also brought into the arena during the display.

In their final cliff assault, 42 Commando Royal Marines took on two targets in a display entitled "Ice and Sand", abseiling and parachuting into the arena, half were dressed in white snow suits and half in dessert combats. The royal standard on the backcloth was moved to one side to reveal the "Last Cliff." Their mission this year was to rescue a female hostage, they assaulted their cliff and neutralised their target one final time. The dramatic extraction of the Marines included abseiling back down the cliff and a series of 'death slides' the highest from the roof of Earls Court where the hostage was brought back to safety. Major Nick Arding, RM took the salute before the Commandos disappeared back into the darkness for the final time.

The Royal Air Force display began with continuity drill by the Queen's Colour Squadron under the direction of Squadron Leader M. Luton. The Central Band of the Royal Air Force under the direction of Wing Commander R.K. Wiffin played 'Parade of the Charioteers' by Miklós Rózsa to accompany the display.

As the 64 members of the QCS fired their SA80 rifles at the end of their display, the RAF Motor Sports Association sped into the arena. The officer in charge, Flt Lt Brian Whatson was driven into the arena in a Ford Escort Mexico rally car, closely followed by two Ford Focus. The arena party setup a series of obstacles including ramps, jumps, seesaw, and bollards. The Focus drivers, raced against each other around the obstacle course, which included jumping one car over the other in the centre of the arena.

* * *

For those who attended the final performance on the evening of Monday 2 August, there was surprise addition to the performance. The arena was in total darkness when the familiar voice of commentator Basil Reitz introduced Colonel Blackadder of the "Royal Regiment of Shirkers." This had been the best kept secret of the Tournament and caught the audience and the majority of the Tournament staff completely unawares. Rowan Atkinson in full military dress, swagger stick under his arm, marched out from the tunnel under the Royal Box to the centre of the arena, halted, and about turned to face the audience.

51 - Rowan Atkinson as Blackadder at the last performance of the Royal Tournament

Under the spotlight, he delivered a monologue to the 12,500 strong, sell-out crowd. This was in the days before mobile phones and social media, and the audience sat in stunned silence as Blackadder started to speak, before roaring with laughter and cheering a few seconds later as the content of the speech became clear.

I'm not aware of any recordings of this part of the show, although a similar monologue was delivered at the Royal Variety Performance the following year. Maj Micheal Parker later revealed that the script had been written by Ben Elton and said that it had been edited somewhat before the final version was approved.

In his speech, Blackadder remarked that Britain led the world in the dismantling of obsolete military equipment, carrying them over obstacles, and reassembling them. Blackadder went on to suggest that that invading France could have helped establish the country on the world stage again, and that everyone in the audience could join the invasion on the Eurostar from Waterloo!

On what could have been a very sombre occasion, this moment of comic genius from the combined talent of Rowan Atkinson and Ben Elton, lifted the mood of the audience, performers, and the Tournament staff. It has gone down in the history of the show as one of the highlights from the Last Run. Remembered fondly by those who were there on the night.

* * *

The arena doors opened one last time on Major Douglas's cue, with stage smoke billowing and backlit in white light, the King's Troop Royal Horse Artillery led the cast into the darkened arena. As with the 1999 opening, the entire King's Troop took part in the Finale on the Queen's night and at the last performance. The six guns, with their officers and outriders paused briefly before slowly making their way to the Warwick Road end. They gave an "eyes right" as they passed the Royal Box and slowly made their way out of the building via the carpeted route through the exhibition area.

The Mounted Band of the Blues and Royals (RHG/D) and the Household Cavalry Musical Ride followed as the House Band, The King's Division Normandy Band under the direction of Captain K. Hatton played the atmospheric theme from the film '1492: Conquest of Paradise' by Vangelis.

The volume increased as the Tri-Service Massed Bands made their way into the arena under the direction of Lieutenant Colonel Richard Waterer, RM accompanied by the flags of all the nations that had taken part in the Tournament over its long history, carried by members of 5th Regiment Royal

Artillery who provided the Support Unit in 1999. A Tri-Service Choir were stationed on the platform over the arena doors, directed by Captain S. Barnwell. A fanfare team, Royal Marines Corps of Drums, and Massed Pipes & Drums completed the musical contingent.

The Field Gun Crews entered the arena to huge cheers from the audience as they took their position for the Finale which was titled "Into the Future". They were by joined by 42 Commando Royal Marines, the Queen's Colour Squadron, and detachments from the Support Unit.

The Massed Bands played a new arrangement by WO2 Michael McDermott, RM, entitled "The Ultimate Battle". This brought together musical excerpts from many of the Finale's of the Micheal Parker era including 1812 Overture, Battle of Trafalgar The Planets, The Battle of Britain, The Armada, and the Battle of Waterloo. As they played, riders from the White Helmets circle the arena, each bike carrying a passenger in a caricature outfit of a historic figure; Nelson, Drake, Wellington, etc. each waving to the audience as they passed.

The hymn 'Now the Day is Over' (Barnby) followed, sung by the Tri-Service Choir accompanied by the vast Massed Bands. As the 100 m^2 LED screen mounted within the background showed a sunset, a list of all the conflicts which the Armed Forces had been involve in between 1880 and 1999 scrolled across the screen. Commentator, Basil Reitz remarked that there had only been one year (1968) in the 20th Century when a member of the Armed Forces had not been killed on active service. The audience and cast, joined in a moment of reflection for all the servicemen and servicewomen who had made the ultimate sacrifice, a reminder that the arena performers at every Tournament had always returned to their role of defending the nation after their short time in the spotlight.

The mood was lifted again as the Massed Bands played the patriotic 'Britannic Salute' (Arne/Elgar) featuring 'Rule Britania' and 'Land of Hope and Glory'. A huge Union Flag unfurled above the Massed bands bringing the entire audience to their feet, joining in a chorus of "Auld Lang Syne" (the traditional song of farewell) before singing the National Anthem as the show drew to a close.

Basil Reitz gave his final announcement as commentator "The 1999 Royal Tournament says, Goodbye!". The audience stood, cheered, and clapped at every show of the Last Run as the performers made their way from the arena at the end of each performance. The March Off music included:

'Good-bye-ee!' (Weston/Lee) 'Tri-Service March Past', 'We're No' Awa' Tae Bide Awa', and "Black Bear". In previous years, some audience members would have left their seats a few minutes early, perhaps to get back to the carpark or rushing for a train, but in 1999, that didn't seem so obvious. Most people, caught up in the moment, wanted to clap every performer as they left the arena. The last to leave the arena were the Massed Pipes & Drums,

52 - Finale of the Royal Tournament 1999

making their way through the arena doors and back into Earls Court Two for the final time.

Raffety and Burnaby could not have imagined that their Grand Military Tournament and Assault-at-Arms at the Agricultural Hall in June 1880 would have gone on to entertain the public for 120 years. Although the world had gone through massive change during that period, the annual Tournament had been a constant in many people's lives. It had continued to promote Skill-at-Arms right up to the end and had raised considerable sums of money to support the Armed Forces Charities.

But perhaps more importantly, the Royal Tournament had brought the Armed Forces closer to the public than ever before or since, demonstrating their skill, courage, enthusiasm, and professionalism. Countless young men and women (myself included) were inspired by their experience at the

Tournament, to join the Armed Forces as regulars or reserves, proud to wear a uniform and serve their Country. A legacy which all those involved in the show would be proud of.

* * *

The Royal Tournament Team gathered one final time in December 1999 for a Royal Reception at St James's Palace in the presence of HRH Princess Alexandra. This provided an opportunity to celebrate the 120-year history of the Tournament and recall the many wonderful memories of the Tournament years.

POSTSCRIPT ONE – A NEW MILLENIUM

In September 1998 Defence Secretary George Robertson had announced to Parliament that the 1999 Royal Tournament would be the last. He said "my aim is to make it more relevant and modern, whilst retaining an element of pageantry." On 20 July 1999, the Evening Herald (Plymouth) reported on the MOD plans for replacing the Tournament: "Next year a spectacular one-off Royal Military Tattoo 2000 will be held at Horse Guards Parade in London – instead of the Royal Tournament." Going on to say, "From 2001 there will be a new tattoo each year within the parade and a new annual military festival, which will move from year to year". The MOD used the umbrella title "Defence 2000" for the proposed series of events to replace the Tournament.

The first part of the MOD Plan came to fruition in July 2000, produced by Major Micheal Parker with an organising committee chaired by Major General Sir Evelyn Webb-Carter. A few of the Royal Tournament team also crossed over to Horse Guards Parade to deliver RMT2000.

The show was the Ministry of Defence's principal contribution to the Millennium celebrations. A vast temporary arena was built on Horse Guards, however unlike the seats for the annual Queen's Birthday Parade which faced the Guards Memorial and St James's Park, the grandstands for RMT2000 faced the Horse Guards Building. The building itself would become a part of the show.

Each performance began at 2100 hrs with a 30-minute traditional Tattoo including: Massed Corps of Drums and a single drummer in 18th Century uniform in a nod to the history of the word 'Tattoo', A tri-service parachute jump, by the Royal Navy Raiders, Red Devils from the Army, and RAF Falcons followed by the 64 members of the Queen's Colour Squadron entering the arena from the Horse Guards Arch to give their display of continuity drill. As an outdoor event, the tattoo also included a series of flypasts from the; Red Arrows, Lancaster Bomber, VC10, Jaguar, and Eurofighter as well as Sea King, Chinook, Merlin, Puma, and Apache helicopters.

The Flying Gunners Motorcycle Display Team from the Royal Artillery, provided a breathtaking performance, culminating in 4-car jump. As the Flying Gunners left the arena, the King's Troop Royal Horse Artillery entered and delivered a spectacular Musical Drive, in the larger arena, the traditional six-gun teams were joined by outriders and mounted officers. The six guns of King's Troop fired a salute to signify the end of the traditional tattoo.

Arena commentator Simon Brooks-Ward introduced the second part of the performance; "Defence of the Realm." The full 18th Century Band entered the arena to the traditional tune "Lillibullero" (Henry Purcell), they were joined by the Tri-Service Massed Bands under the direction of Lieutenant Colonel Richard Waterer, RM.

53 - The King's Troop RHA at the Royal Military Tattoo 2000

Two temporary walls were erected in front of the Horse Guards Building, painted to appear to be part of the building design, they could open in various places to allow musicians and performers to enter and exit the arena. In front of this walls were two large LED screens, mounted on tracks, they could be joined together in front of the Horse Guards Arch to create a single big screen or moved apart to create two separate screens, as the content of the show required. The choir of The Lucknow Band of The Prince of Wales's Division were also stood in front of screens, on the moving platforms.

The Royal Tournament had pushed the boundaries of technology for events and RMT2000 continued that tradition. As the sun set each evening, high powered projectors mounted on the lighting gantries above the grandstand began to project onto the historic Horse Guards Building creating the ultimate 'Son et lumière'.

The Defence of the Realm pageant told the story of more than a thousand years of British Military history, from Viking Invaders through to Peacekeeping in the year 2000. The show was one of the most technically advanced ever staged in the UK, with over 1,000 years of history packed into an hour-long performance, Maj Parker joked "if you missed your cue, you could end up in the wrong century!"

Celebrity guest voices included household names such as Anthony Andrews, Dame Judi Dench, Hannah Gordon, Robert Hardy, Prunella Scales, Timothy West, Edward Woodward, and Kate Adie. Each voicing characters from historic timeline who were depicted by performers in costumes of the character or period they were representing.

The performance included Alfred the Great, a Tudor joust the Union of the Crowns of England and Scotland, the Civil War and Restoration of the Monarchy, the Battle of Trafalgar, Waterloo, the Crimean War, Boer War, The Great War and the birth of the Royal Air Force, as well as World War Two. It then moved on to more recent memories such as The Cold War, Northern Ireland, the Fall of the Berlin Wall, and the First Gulf War.

The Finale Brought together all of the historic characters as they marched through history from Horse Guards Arch to the tunnel under the Royal Box. Detachments of current serving men and women of the three Armed Services also marched forward, some in uniform, some in sports or adventurous training kit, showing the diversity of roles and opportunities in the services.

The Finale theme was "A Force for Good in the World" linked to the UK's role in the United Nations and recent Peacekeeping Operations. As the full cast assembled, the Massed Bands played 'I Vow to thee, My Country' (Holst) with Dame Judi Dench reading words of the poem of the same name by Sir Cecil Spring Rice.

The show ran for a week, with members of the Royal Family attending each evening, the then Prime Minister Tony Blair also made the short journey from Downing Street to watch a performance. Her Majesty Queen Elizabeth occupied the Royal Box on the Thursday evening.

54 - Finale of the Royal Military Tattoo 2000

The show closed on the Saturday evening and was followed by a party to thank the participants at Chelsea Barracks later that evening. The team regrouped at Horse Guards the following week to deliver the Queen

Mother's 100th Birthday Pageant (QM100). Her Majesty Queen Elizabeth The Queen Mother arrived in an open carriage accompanied by HRH The Prince of Wales. The Massed Bands played the National Anthem as a Guard of Honour made up of all the Military Units which The Queen Mother was associated with gave a Royal Salute.

The Queen Mother reviewed the ranks of the assembled parade from her carriage before making her way to the coved Dias where she was welcomed by Major General Sir Evelyn Webb-Carter, Chairman of the organising committee. The Queen Mother then stood while the parade, led by the Royal Navy contingent, march passed.

The procession which followed, was a celebration of her life, it included representatives of all the charities of which she was patron. She continued to stand and wave as camels, horses, dancers, vintage vehicles, and all manner of performers passed the dais. The entire parade assembled in front of Her Majesty and gave three cheers as rose petals (dropped by Gurkhas from the lighting gantry) fluttered down over the invited audience from the organisations that Her Majesty was involved with. A fitting tribute to a lifetime of service.

As Raffety had reused the seating and arena from the Horse Show at the Agricultural Hall for the first Tournaments in the 1880s, over a century later the organisers were again 'sweating the assets' by using a similar setup for RMT2000 and QM100. Both events had been a huge success in their own right.

The following spring, in response to a question from Lord Stoddart of Swindon on 9 March 2001, the Hansard of the House of Lords records that Baroness Symons of Vernham Dean said, "We intend to identify possible future occasions where an event on the scale of RMT2000 would be both appropriate and practicable." The annual Tattoo on Horse Guards promised as part of Defence 2000 has never happened.

An International Festival of the Sea (IFOS) was staged in Portsmouth in 2001. In 2002 the annual Firepower Demonstration held at The Royal School of Artillery at Larkhill in Wiltshire was opened to the public for one year only under the name "Army 2002". The Royal Air Force nominated The Royal International Air Tattoo (RIAT) as "Defence 2003", this was postponed to 2004 due to operational commitments (although RIAT went ahead).

On 30 January 2004 the Hansard records a statement from Ivor Caplin, Parliamentary Under-Secretary of State for Defence: "On 1 September 2003 I informed the House that the Defence 2003 exhibition, under the leadership of the Royal Air force, which was scheduled to take place at the Royal International Air Tattoo, had been postponed by 12 months because of operational pressures" he went on to say "In light of the continued high level of operational commitments and the associated demands upon service personnel and their families, the Ministry of Defence has now concluded that Defence 2004 should not take place.

The "Defence 2000" brand was not used again.

* * *

In 2007, the Royal Navy Field Gun Associations arranged an event to mark the centenary of the first Inter-Command Field Gun Competition, staged at Olympia in 1907. The Command 100 Dinner was staged at the Painted Hall, Greenwich by an organising committee led by former Devonport Field Gunner Lieutenant Commander 'Grassy' Meadows. Each of the three rows of tables of the historic Painted Hall were allocated to one of the Commands (Portsmouth, Devonport, and Fleet Air Arm), there were also a few ex-Field Gunners who had run for Chatham.

Before dinner was served, Basil Reitz (former Commentator at the Royal Tournament) read the names of the members of the Naval Brigade who had died in the Relief of Ladysmith in 1899. The Inter-Command Field Gun Competition had been inspired by the exploits of the Naval Brigade in the Relief of Ladysmith, for those present who had dedicated their lives to honouring the memory of those who had taken part in the relief, this was a something of a poignant moment.

I had the pleasure of sitting next to Basil at dinner that night. There was a steady stream of ex-Field Gunners who came to the table during the evening to meet the man himself, some asked for photographs, some to have their menu's signed, others just wanted to shake his hand. Basil had commentated on the Royal Tournament for over 40 years, all but the oldest of the ex-Field Gunners in the room had heard his unique voice commentating on their runs at 'The Court'. But few, had ever seen, let alone met the man behind the voice. on hearing him read the role of honour from Ladysmith, many of the ex-Field Gunners were moved to tears.

* * *

A reunion lunch was held during the summer of 2009, marking ten years since the Last Run. Organised by Major George Douglas, Arena Master of the Royal Tournament from 1981 to 1999 and of the Royal Military Tattoo 2000, needless to say the organisation was excellent. The lunch was held in the Officers Mess at Wellington Barracks, a short walk from the final home of the Tournament office. The occasion gave an opportunity to reminisce and catch up with former colleagues.

POSTSCRIPT TWO – A NEW START

Following his retirement from the Army in 2001, Major General Sir Evelyn Webb-Carter was appointed as the Chief Executive of the Army Benevolent Fund (later rebranded as ABF The Soldiers' Charity) in 2002. Fundraising events were key to the Charity's strategy however the ABF did not have a Flagship Event to anchor its strategy on.

Former Life Guards Officer turned Event Producer; Chrsitopher Joll approached Sir Evelyn with a suggestion to create a new event for the charity in 2008. The new show would be based on format of the Royal Tournament. World renowned entertainment management company: IMG were also brought in to support the delivery under the direction of Executive Producer Stephen Flintwood.

Two London venues were initially considered for the event, The O2 and Earls Court. After careful consideration, Earls Court was chosen, as the venue had been designed to stage the Royal Tournament (amongst other events) in the 1930s. The next consideration was the name of the show, the Royal title had been awarded when Queen Victoria became patron of the Grand Military Tournament in 1883, as this was to be a new venture it would not be possible to revive the name. Several options of names were put forward; however, it was considered that the name should include the word "Tournament" given the close connections with the pre-1999 show and so the British Military Tournament was born.

Agreement was reached with the MOD to stage the event in 2010, on the condition that it did not clash with the Armed Forces Day National Event to be staged in Cardiff on 26 June. The only period available at Earls Court with sufficient time to allow for the building of seats, rigging, and installation of the arena surface was from 30 November to 6 December. The Royal Tournament had traditionally been a summer show, however BMT would be a winter one (the snowfall over the London and the Southeast of England on the night of 1 December added an additional level of complexity to the event!).

Following the old theatre saying, "The show must go on", Nick Mattingley (Production Director) and David Edwards (Technical Manager) ensured that the arena build, accommodation setup, and rehearsal schedule remained on track in spite of the winter weather. As with the Royal Tournament, the area behind the stalls seating at Earls Court was transformed into a temporary exhibition space including sponsor and charity stands as well as static displays from the Armed Forces.

The MOD agreed to provide service personnel for the arena displays and the static displays in the exhibition area for BMT. Rather than requesting a team of Military Ushers (as had been the tradition for the Royal Tournament), we recruited a team of 200 Volunteer 'Show Makers'. Under the direction of Jim Kemp, these wonderful volunteers (including most of my own family!) donated their time to support the event each year, checking tickets at the entrances, showing guests to their seats, supporting guests with mobility issues, and providing wayfaring support.

55 - King's Troop Royal Horse Artillery at the British Military Tournament

The theme for the first BMT was the story of the Army from the Civil War to the modern day. Each performance included a Musical Drive by the King's Troop Royal Horse Artillery, Gymnastic display by the Royal Army Physical Training Corps, the Light Cavalry and Company of Pikemen and Musketeers from the Honourable Artillery Company, the Household Cavalry Mounted Regiment, and the Massed Bands (Grenadier Guards, Coldstream Guards, Scots Guards, The Rifles, and Brigade of Gurkhas all under the direction of Lieutenant Colonel Graham Jones). Members of the National Theatre performed an extract from War Horse by Michael Morpurgo.

* * *

There was a desire to include a Field Gun Competition, however the Royal Navy were no longer supporting Command Field Gun (as seen at the Royal Tournament) so an alternative was sought. The Combined Cadet Corps of Wellington College in Berkshire have been running their own Field Gun since 1984. It was introduced by Lieutenant-Commander Simon Braidwood who was responsible for the Naval Section of the Wellington College CCF from 1977 to 1989. The first demonstration run was staged on the South Front of the College in October 1984, performed again on Speech Day the following year. The tradition continues with crews running on Speech Day each May.

The current Trainers at Wellington are former Fleet Air Arm Field Gunners; Kev Clarke and Jim Harwood who give up their time each year to train the student volunteers aged between 14 and 18. The crews learn Command Field Gun Drill, using scaled down guns and limber but compete over the same size obstacles as the Crews did at the Royal Tournament (5ft walls and 28ft chasm).

56 - Wellington College Field Gun, British Military Tournament

Marquees were erected at the school to enable the crews to train in the autumn term rather than the summer term, ready for the performances in December. The two crews were named Terrible and Powerful, in honour of two Royal Navy Ships which were instrumental in the Relief of Ladysmith on the suggestion of Mike Bell, former Portsmouth B Crew Field Gunner and later WO1 in charge of the ARRC Display at the 1994 Royal Tournament.

*　　*　　*

From 2011, the Royal Navy & Royal Marines Charity and Royal Air Force Benevolent Fund also joined the BMT, and so The Band of HM Royal Marines, Commando Training Centre Royal Marines and The Central Band of The Royal Air Force both joined the cast for the second year. The theme of the 2011 BMT was Britain's 'Special Relationship' with the United States of America. Performers included 4th Battalion, 3rd U.S. Infantry Regiment (The Old Guard), the U.S. Army Drill Team, and U.S. Army Band Europe as well as American Civil War re-enactment society, Southern Skirmish Association (SoSkAn). Her Majesty Queen Elizabeth II attended the Friday Evening Performance.

Major General Sir Evelyn Webb-Carter had been the driving force behind the BMT, he retired from ABF The Soldiers' Charity in 2012 with Maj Gen

Martin Rutledge taking over as Chief Executive. Brigadier Robin Bacon, Chief of Staff for the Charity took over the role of Chairman of BMT, supported by an experienced team from the ABF including Stephen Grogan (Head of Events) and Sophie Lindsay (now Coad) (Event Manager). Marking the Diamond Jubilee of Her Majesty Queen Elizabeth II, the 2012 theme was the 'Life and Times of The Queen'.

The theme for 2013 was 'Legends & Heroes', the show opened with an inflatable depiction of German submarine U-559 in the centre of the arena as the cast recreated the legendary capture of the German Enigma Code Books enabling the decryption of the code at Bletchley Park. Other displays included Heroes such as Horatio Nelson (Battle of Trafalgar) and T.E. Lawrence (Arab Revolt). Each performance of the British Military Tournament ended with a Muster, the entire cast formed up in the arena, with the Guest of Honour taking the salute before the March off. Initially in 2010 this was based on Britannia's Muster which had been part of the 1910 Royal Tournament and became the traditional Finale for the BMT.

The final performance of BMT took place on the afternoon of Sunday 8 December 2013, the show had run for four years and attracted audiences of up to 45,000 per year, raising funds and generating awareness of the work of the three main Armed Forces Charities. With uncertainty about the future of Earls Court, the charities took the decision not to request the military assets required to stage the British Military Tournament the following year. Demolition work started on Earls Court in December 2014.

POSTSCRIPT THREE – A NIGHT TO REMEMBER

Marking the 25th Anniversary of the last Royal Tournament, a concert was staged at The Royal Military Chapel, The Guards' Chapel on the evening of 2 October 2024. The concert was performed by The Band of the Royal Yeomanry (Inns of Court and City Yeomanry) under the direction of Major David Hammond. Proceeds from the concert were given to SSAFA, the Armed Forces charity.

The musical programme was drawn from across the 120-year history of the Tournament. The Concert opened with 'Music for a Tournament' composed by Captain (later Lt. Col) Trevor Sharpe for the 1963 Tournament. Maj Gen Evelyn Webb-Carter welcomed the audience and introduced the band. The programme also included 'Gavotte' from the 1866 Opera Mignon, which was played on the first day of the first Tournament in 1880 by the Band of the Royal Engineers. On this occasion, it provided the accompaniment for a display of fencing provided by the Army Fencing Union in a recreation of the first combat at the Agricultural Hall at the Grand Military Tournament and Assault at Arms.

57 - Fencers from the Army Fencing Union at the 25th Anniversary Concert

Music from the RAF Years followed, introduced by Lynne Parsons, former Press Office Assistant at the Tournament. This section included the themes from 'Thunderbirds' and 'The Great Escape,' and the 'RAF March Past'. The band also played the music from the Musical Drive followed by 'The Life Guards Slow March' and 'The Blues & Royals Slow March' marking the numerous musical rides which were performed at the Tournament over the years.

The first half of the programme concluded with 'The Olympic Spirit' by John Williams, acknowledging the origins of the Tournament as a series of competitions and noting some of the competitors who went on to compete in the Olympic Games. This was introduced by Jarrod Steadman, Curator of the Royal Army Physical Training Corps Museum.

The second half of the concert opened with a piece of music commission by the Royal Tournament Committee, Royal Tournament, Op 115 which was composed by Derek Bourgeois in 1989. The band then performed the music from the music from the Royal Navy Field Gun Competition including: 'When I was a Lad' & 'For a British Tar' from H.M.S. Pinafore, 'Heart of Oak', 'Ship Ahoy!' (All the Nice Girls Love a Sailor), and 'Jack the Lad' (Hornpipe). Mike Bell, former Portsmouth Field Gunner, introduced this section, sharing memories from the 1970 Field Gun Competition.

58 - The Band of the Royal Yeomanry and Piper Callum Hall

Catie Bland, former Personal Assistant to Major Micheal Parker introduced 'Highland Cathedral' which had been performed by the Massed Bands, Pipes & Drums of the Royal Air Force during the Finale of the 1998 Tournament. The band were joined by Piper Callum Hall from The London Scottish Pipes & Drums.

The finale of the concert included '1812 Overture', 'I Vow to Thee My Country', and 'Last Post and Lead Kindly Light' followed by 'God Save the King'. Rowan Atkinson introduced the finale, recalling the final performance of the Royal Tournament in 1999 when he addressed the sell-out crowd as Blackadder.

The traditional end to the Tournament each year was the 'March Off' as the various performers left the arena after the show. Following that tradition, the band played three marches to finish the performance. 'The Farmer's Boy', the Regimental March of the Royal Yeomanry followed by the Regimental March of the 'Queen's Own Hussars' in memory of Major Micheal Parker. Ending with 'The Army the Navy and the Air Force.'

59 - Rowan Atkinson introducing the Anniversary Concert Finale

Hearing the music from the Royal Tournament and the stories of the people behind the show brought back many happy memories, and the odd tear to the eye. The concert was truly "a night to remember."

APPENDIX A – TOURNAMENT CHAIRMEN

Honorary Secretary

1880 - 1881	Major General Edwyn Sherard Burnaby, M.P.

Chairman

1882	Prince Edward of Saxe-Weimar KP GCB GCH GCVO
1883	Major-General Sir George Higginson GCB GCVO
1884 - 1888	Major-General Sir Reginald Gipps GCB
1889 - 1895	Prince Edward of Saxe-Weimar KP GCB GCH GCVO
1896 - 1897	Major-General The Lord Methuen GCB GCMG GCVO
1898 - 1902	Major-General Sir Henry Trotter, GCVO, DL
1903 - 1906	Major-General L. J. Oliphant C.V.O., C.B
1907 - 1909	Major-General Hon. Sir F. W. Stopford, K.C.M.G., C.B.
1910 - 1913	Major-General A. E. Codrington, C.V.O., C.B.
1914	Major-General Sir F. Llody, K.C.B., C.V.O., D.S.O.
1919	Major-General Sir G. P. T. Feilding, K.C.B., C.M.G., D.S.O.
1920 - 1923	Major-General G. D. Jeffreys, C.B., C.M.G.
1924 - 1927	Major-General The Lord Ruthven, C.B., C.M.G., D.S.O.
1928 - 1931	Major-General Sir Charles Corkran, KCVO CB CMG
1932	Major-General Albemarle Cator, CB DSO
1933 - 1934	Major-General Sir Charles Grant, KCB KCVO DSO
1935 - 1938	Major-General Sir Bertram Sergison-Brooke, KCB KCVO CMG DSO
1939	Lieutenant-General Sir Andrew Thorne, KCB CMG DSO
1947 - 1949	Major-General Sir John Marriott, KCVO CB DSO MC
1950 - 1953	Major-General Sir Julian Gascoigne, KCMG KCVO CB DSO
1954 - 1957	Major-General Sir George Johnson, KCVO CB CBE DSO
1958 - 1959	Major-General Sir Rodney Moore, GCVO KCB CBE DSO
1960 - 1962	Major-General Sir George Burns, GCVO CB DSO OBE MC
1963 - 1965	Major-General Sir John Nelson, KCVO CB DSO OBE MC
1966 - 1967	Major-General Sir Basil Eugster, KCB KCVO CBE DSO MC
1968 - 1971	Major-General Lord Michael Fitzalan-Howard, GCVO CB CBE MC
1972 - 1973	Major-General Sir James Bowes-Lyon, GCVO CB OBE MC
1974 - 1976	Major-General Sir Philip Ward, KCVO CB
1977 - 1979	Major-General Sir John Swinton, KCVO OBE
1980 - 1982	Major-General Sir Desmond Langley, KCVO MBE
1983 - 1985	Major-General Sir James Eyre, KCVO CBE
1986 - 1988	Major-General Sir Christopher Airy, KCVO CBE
1989 - 1990	Major-General Sir Simon Cooper, GCVO

1991 - 1993	Major-General Sir Robert Corbett, KCVO CB
1994 - 1996	Major-General Sir Iain Mackay-Dick, KCVO MBE
1997 - 1999	Major-General Sir Evelyn Webb-Carter, KCVO OBE

APPENDIX B – MUSICAL RIDE PERFORMANCES

1882	Musical Double Ride	1st Life Guards
1883	Musical Ride	2nd Life Guards
1884	Musical Ride	1st Life Guards
1885	Musical Ride	Royal Horse Guards
1886	Musical Ride	2nd Life Guards
1887	Musical Ride	1st Life Guards
1888	Musical Ride	Royal Horse Guards
1889	Musical Ride	12th (Prince of Wales's) Royal Lancers
1890	Musical Ride	1st Life Guards Lothians Berwickshire Yeomanry Cavalry
1891	Musical Ride	Royal Horse Guards
1892	Musical Double Ride	17th (The Duke of Cambridge's Own) Lancers
1893	Musical Ride	2nd Life Guards
1894	Musical Ride	1st Life Guards
1895	Musical Ride	Royal Horse Guards
1896	Musical Ride	Royal Scots Greys 2nd Life Guards
1897	Musical Ride	3rd Dragoon Guards 1st Life Guards
1898	Musical Ride	Royal Horse Guards 7th (Princess Royal's) Dragoon Guards
1899	Musical Ride	1st (Royal) Dragoons
1900	Musical Ride	2nd Life Guards
1901	Musical Ride	1st Life Guards 21st Lancers
1902	Musical Ride	Royal Horse Guards
1903	Musical Double Ride	2nd Life Guards
1904	Musical Ride	1st Life Guards 21st Lancers
1905	Musical Double Ride	Royal Horse Guards
1906	Musical Ride	2nd Life Guards
1907	Musical Double Ride	1st Life Guards
1908	Musical Double Ride	1st Life Guards
1909	Musical Ride	Royal Horse Guards 3rd Dragoon Guards
1910	Musical Ride	21st (Empress of India's) Lancers
1911	Musical Ride	1st Life Guards Royal Scots Greys

1912	Musical Ride	Royal Horse Guards 3rd Hussars
1913	Musical Ride	2nd Life Guards 18th Hussars
1914	Musical Double Ride	1st Life Guards
1919	Musical Ride	Saumur Cavalry School (France)
1920	Musical Double Ride	Royal Horse Guards
1921	Musical Ride	2nd Life Guards
1922	Musical Ride	1st Life Guards
1923	Musical Ride	12th (Prince of Wales's) Royal Lancers
1924	Musical Ride	13/18th Hussars
1925	Musical Ride	Life Guards (1st and 2nd)
1926	Musical Ride	10th Royal Hussars (P.W.O.)
1927	Musical Ride	Royal Horse Guards
1928	Musical Ride	Royal Scots Greys (2nd Dragoons)
1929	Musical Ride	17th/21st Lancers
1930	Musical Ride	3rd Carabineers (Prince of Wales's Dragoon Guards)
1932	Musical Ride	Queen's Bays
1933	Musical Double Ride	Life Guards
1934	Musical Ride	Royal Horse Guards
1935	Musical Ride	9th Queen's Royal Lancers
1936	Musical Ride	3rd Carabineers (Prince of Wales's Dragoon Guards)
1937	Musical Ride	16th/5th Lancers
1938	Musical Ride	Royal Scots Greys (2nd Dragoons)
1939	Musical Ride	Life Guards
1948	Musical Ride	Household Cavalry
1949	Musical Ride	Household Cavalry
1950	Musical Ride	Household Cavalry
1951	Musical Ride	Household Cavalry
1952	Musical Ride	Household Cavalry
1953	Musical Ride	Royal Canadian Mounted Police
1954	Musical Ride	Household Cavalry
1955	Musical Ride	Household Cavalry
1957	Musical Ride	Household Cavalry
1958	Musical Ride	Household Cavalry
1961	Musical Ride	Household Cavalry
1964	Musical Ride	Household Cavalry
1969	Musical Ride	Royal Canadian Mounted Police

1970	Musical Ride	Household Cavalry
1972	Musical Ride	Household Cavalry
1974	Quadrille	Household Cavalry
1978	Quadrille	Household Cavalry
1980	Quadrille	Household Cavalry
1987	Musical Ride	Danish Guard Husar
1988	Musical Ride	Household Cavalry
1991	Musical Ride	Household Cavalry
1997	Musical Ride	Household Cavalry
1999	Musical Ride	Household Cavalry

APPENDIX C – MUSICAL DRIVE PERFORMANCES

	Royal Military Tournament		
1896	"D" Battery	Royal Horse Artillery	
1897	"G" Battery	Royal Horse Artillery	
1898	"G" Battery	Royal Horse Artillery	
1899	"G" Battery	Royal Horse Artillery	
1900	"N" Battery	Royal Horse Artillery	
1901	"V" Battery	Royal Horse Artillery	
1902	"X" Battery	Royal Horse Artillery	
1903	"X" Battery	Royal Horse Artillery	
1904	"X" Battery	Royal Horse Artillery	
	Royal Naval & Military Tournament		
1905	"Y" Battery	Royal Horse Artillery	
1906	"Y" Battery	Royal Horse Artillery	
1907	"A" Battery	Royal Horse Artillery	The Chestnut Troop
1908	"A" Battery	Royal Horse Artillery	The Chestnut Troop
1909	"BB" Battery	Royal Horse Artillery	
1910	"BB" Battery	Royal Horse Artillery	
1911	"BB" Battery	Royal Horse Artillery	
1912	"F" Battery	Royal Horse Artillery	
1913	"F" Battery	Royal Horse Artillery	
1914	"F" Battery	Royal Horse Artillery	
1915 - 18	No Tournament		
	Royal Naval, Military & Air Force Tournament		
1919	"AA" Battery	Royal Horse Artillery	
	Royal Tournament		
1920	No Musical Drive		
1921	"N" Battery	Royal Horse Artillery	Eagle Troop
1922	"O" Battery	Royal Horse Artillery	
1923	No Musical Drive		
1924	"O" Battery	Royal Horse Artillery	Rocket Troop
1925[29]	"O" Battery	Royal Horse Artillery	Rocket Troop
1926	"O" Battery	Royal Horse Artillery	
1927	"M" Battery	Royal Horse Artillery	

[29] The Musical Drive formed part of the Grand Pageant "UBIQUE" – A Pageant of the Royal Artillery.

1928	"M" Battery	Royal Horse Artillery	
1929	"M" Battery	Royal Horse Artillery	
1930	"J" Battery	Royal Horse Artillery	
1931	"J" Battery	Royal Horse Artillery	
1932	"J" Battery	Royal Horse Artillery	
1933	"F" Battery	Royal Horse Artillery	
1934	"F" Battery	Royal Horse Artillery	
1935	"F" Battery	Royal Horse Artillery	Sphinx
1936	"F" Battery	Royal Horse Artillery	Sphinx
1937	"K" Battery	Royal Horse Artillery	Sphinx
1938	"K" Battery	Royal Horse Artillery	Sphinx
1939	"K" Battery	Royal Horse Artillery	
1940 - 46	No Tournament		
1947	No Musical Drive		
1948 - 99	The King's Troop	Royal Horse Artillery	

APPENDIX D – MUSICAL PERFORMERS

The following pages list the bands which performed at the Tournament either in the arena or as the resident band. With thanks to Colin Dean for his research.

The Grand Military Tournament 1880
The following bands acted as Resident Band, a different band performing each day:
Band of the Royal Engineers
Band of the Royal Horse Guards
Band of the 1st Life Guards
Band of the 2nd Life Guards
Band of the Coldstream Guards

The Grand Military Tournament 1881
The following bands acted as Resident Band, a different band performing each day:
Band of the 1st Life Guards
Band of the 2nd Life Guards
Band of the 11th Prince Albert's Own Hussars
Band of the Royal Artillery
Band of the Royal Engineers
Band of the Scots Guards
6th Regiment (Royal First Warwickshire)
1st London Artillery Brigade
3rd Middlesex Artillery

The Grand Military Tournament 1882
Band of the 1st Life Guards
Band of the Royal Fusiliers
Band of the 1st Tower Hamlets Volunteers

The Grand Military Tournament 1883
Band of the 2nd Life Guards

The Royal Military Tournament 1884
Band of the 1st Life Guards

The Royal Military Tournament 1885
Band of the Royal Horse Guards

The Royal Military Tournament 1886
Band of the 2nd Life Guards

The Royal Military Tournament 1887
Band of the 1st Life Guards

The Royal Military Tournament 1888
Resident Bands:
Band of the Royal Horse Guards (The Blues)
Band of the Coldstream Guards

The Royal Military Tournament 1889
Resident Bands:
Band of the 2nd Life Guards
Band of the 12th (Prince of Wales's Royal) Lancers
Band of the Royal Artillery (Aldershot Mounted Division)

The Royal Military Tournament 1890
Resident Band:
1st Life Guards

The Royal Military Tournament 1891
Resident Band: Band of the Royal Horse Guards (The Blues)

The Royal Military Tournament 1892
Resident Band: Band of the 17th (Duke of Cambridge's Own) Lancers

The Royal Military Tournament 1893
Resident Band: Band of the 2nd Life Guards

The Royal Military Tournament 1894
Resident Bands: Band of the 1st Life Guards
2nd Dragoons (Royal Scots Greys)

The Royal Military Tournament 1895
Resident Band: Band of the Royal Horse Guards (The Blues)

The Royal Military Tournament 1896
Resident Bands:
Band of the 2nd Life Guards
2nd Dragoons (Royal Scots Greys)

The Royal Military Tournament 1897
Resident Bands:
Band of the 1st Life Guards
Band of the 3rd (Prince of Wales's) Dragoon Guards

The Royal Military Tournament 1898
Resident Bands:
Band of the Royal Horse Guards (The Blues)
7th (Princess Royal's) Dragoon Guards

The Royal Military Tournament 1899
Resident Bands:
Band of the 2nd Life Guards
Band of the 1st (Royal) Dragoons

The Royal Military Tournament 1900
Resident Band: Band of the 2nd Life Guards

The Royal Military Tournament 1901
Resident Bands:
Band of the 2nd Life Guards
Band of the 21st (Empress of India's) Lancers

The Royal Military Tournament 1902
Resident Band: Band of the Royal Horse Guards (The Blues)

The Royal Military Tournament 1903
Resident Bands:
Band of the 2nd Life Guards
Band of the 5th (Royal Irish) Lancers

The Royal Military Tournament 1904
Resident Bands:
Band of the 1st Life Guards
Band of the 21st (Empress of India's) Lancers

The Royal Naval and Military Tournament 1905
Resident Bands:
Band of the Royal Horse Guards (The Blues)
Band of the 16th (The Queen's) Lancers

The Royal Naval and Military Tournament 1906
Resident Band: Band of the 2nd Life Guards

The Royal Naval and Military Tournament 1907
Resident Bands:
Band of the 1st Life Guards
Band of the 16th (The Queen's) Lancers

The Royal Naval and Military Tournament 1908
Buglers of 4th Bn. King's Royal Rifle Corps (60th Rifles)
Resident Band: Band of the 1st Life Guards

The Royal Naval and Military Tournament 1909
Resident Bands:
Band of the Royal Horse Guards (The Blues)
Band of the 3rd (Prince of Wales's) Dragoon Guards

The Royal Naval and Military Tournament 1910
Resident Band: Band of the 21st (Empress of India's) Lancers

The Royal Naval and Military Tournament 1911
Resident Bands:
Band of the 1st Life Guards
Band of the 2nd Dragoons (Royal Scots Greys)

The Royal Naval and Military Tournament 1912
Resident Bands:
Band of the Royal Horse Guards (The Blues)
3rd (King's Own) Hussars
Duke of York's Royal Military School

The Royal Naval and Military Tournament 1913
Resident Band: Band of the 2nd Life Guards
Duke of York's Royal Military School

The Royal Naval and Military Tournament 1914
Resident Bands:
Band of the 1st Life Guards
Band of the 5th (Princess Charlotte of Wales's) Dragoon Guards
The Band of the Duke of York's Royal Military School

The Royal Naval, Military and Air Force Tournament 1919
Resident Band: Band of the Plymouth Division, Royal Marine Light Infantry

The Royal Tournament 1920
Resident Bands:
Band of the Royal Horse Guards (The Blues)
Band of the 17th (Duke of Cambridge's) Lancers

The Royal Tournament 1921
Resident Band: Band of the 2nd Life Guards

The Royal Tournament 1922
Drums and Fife bands from the Brigade of Guards
Resident Band: Band of the 1st Life Guards

The Royal Tournament 1923
1st Bn. Scots Guards
2nd Bn. Scots Guards
2nd Bn. The Royal Scots (The Royal Regiment)
1st Bn. The Cameronians (Scottish Rifles)
1st Bn. The Royal Scots Fusiliers
2nd Bn. The King's Own Scottish Borderers
2nd Bn. The Black Watch (Royal Highlanders)
1st Bn. Seaforth Highlanders (Ross-shire Buffs, The Duke of Albanys')
2nd Bn. The Queen's Own Cameron Highlanders
2nd Bn. The Argyll and Sutherland Highlanders (Princess Louise's)
Drums of:
2nd Bn. The Black Watch (Royal Highlanders)
2nd Bn. The Queen's Own Cameron Highlanders
2nd Bn. The Argyll and Sutherland Highlanders (Princess Louise's)
Resident Band: Band of the 12th Royal Lancers

The Royal Tournament 1924
Band from the Royal Naval School of Music, Eastney
Resident Band: Band of the 13th/18th Hussars

The Royal Tournament 1925
Resident Band: Band of the Royal Artillery

The Royal Tournament 1926
Resident Band: Band of the 10th Hussars (Prince of Wales's Own)

The Royal Tournament 1927
Massed Pipes and Drums:
The Scots Guards
The Royal Scots (The Royal Regiment)
The Royal Scots Fusiliers
The King's Own Scottish Borderers
The Black Watch (Royal Highlanders)
The Highland Light Infantry (City of Glasgow Regiment)
Seaforth Highlanders (Ross-Shire Buffs, The Duke of Albany's)
The Gordon Highlanders
The Queen's Own Cameron Highlanders
The Argyll and Sutherland Highlanders (Princess Louise's)
Resident Bands:
(First week): Band of the Royal Horse Guards (The Blues)
(Second week): Band of the 11th Hussars (Prince Albert's Own)

The Royal Tournament 1928
Band, Pipes and Drums of 1st Bn. Royal Scots Fusiliers
Boys of the Duke of York's Royal Military School

Resident Band: The Royal Scots Greys (2nd Dragoons)

The Royal Tournament 1929
Band and Drums of 1st Bn. The Middlesex Regiment (Duke of Cambridge's Own)
2nd Bn. The Somerset Light Infantry (Prince Albert's)
1st Bn. The Oxfordshire and Buckinghamshire Light Infantry
2nd Bn. The King's Royal Rifle Corps
2nd Bn. The Rifle Brigade (Prince Consort's Own).
Band of the Royal Hospital School, Greenwich
Resident Band: 17th/21st Lancers

The Royal Tournament 1930
2nd Bn. The Royal Fusiliers (City of London Regiment)
Massed Pipes and Drums of the Scots Guards
Resident Band: Band of 3rd Carabiniers (Prince of Wales's Dragoon Guards)

The Royal Tournament 1931
Band and Drums of 2nd Bn. The Gloucestershire Regiment
Band from the Royal Naval School of Music
Pipes and Drums of The London Scottish
Resident Band: 14th/20th Hussars

The Royal Tournament 1932
Band and Drums of 1st Bn. The Prince of Wales's Volunteers
Resident Band: The Band of the Queen's Bays (2nd Dragoon Guards)

The Royal Tournament 1933
Band, Pipes and Drums of 1st Bn. The Royal Scots (The Royal Regiment)
Resident Band: Band of the Life Guards

The Royal Tournament 1934
Band, Pipes and Drums of 2nd Bn. The Black Watch (Royal Highlanders)
Resident Band: Band of the Royal Horse Guards (The Blues)

The Royal Tournament 1935
Band and Drums of 2nd Bn. The Queen's Royal Regiment
Massed Drums and Fifes of 167th Infantry Brigade, Territorial Army (Royal Fusiliers), comprising:
1st, 2nd, 3rd and 4th Battalions City of London Regiment -
Band and Drums of the Duke of York's Royal Military School
Resident Band: Band of the 9th Queen's Royal Lancers

The Royal Tournament 1936
Band and Drums of 2nd Bn. The Royal Norfolk Regiment
Resident Band: Band of 3rd Carabiniers (Prince of Wales's Dragoon Guards)

The Royal Tournament 1937
The Band of the Royal Marines composite band from Chatham, Portsmouth and Plymouth Divisions
Band of the Duke of York's Royal Military School
Resident Band: The Band of the 16th/5th Lancers

The Royal Tournament 1938
Mounted Band of the Royal Scots Greys (2nd Dragoons)
Massed Pipes and Drums:
1st Bn. Scots Guards
2nd Bn. Scots Guards
2nd Bn. The Cameronians (Scottish Rifles)
Depot, The Cameronians (Scottish Rifles)
1st Bn. The Highland Light Infantry (City of Glasgow Regiment)
Depot, The Highland Light Infantry (City of Glasgow Regiment)
2nd Bn. Seaforth Highlanders (Ross-Shire Buffs, The Duke of Albany's)
1st Bn. The Queen's Own Cameron Highlanders
Band of the Royal Air Force

Resident Bands:
The Band of the 5th Royal Inniskilling Dragoon Guards
The Band of the Royal Scots Greys (2nd Dragoons)

The Royal Tournament 1939
The Band of H.M. Royal Marines (Chatham Division)
Band of the Royal Air Force
Band of the Duke of York's Royal Military School
Resident Band: The Band of the Life Guards

The Royal Tournament 1947
Massed Pipes and Drums
Scots Guards
The Royal Scots (The Royal Regiment)
The Black Watch (Royal Highland Regiment)
The Highland Light Infantry (City of Glasgow Regiment)
Seaforth Highlanders (Ross-Shire Buffs, The Duke of Albany's)
The Gordon Highlanders
The Queen's Own Cameron Highlanders
The Argyll and Sutherland Highlanders (Princess Louise's)
The Band of H.M. Royal Marines (Chatham Group)
Central Band of the Royal Air Force
The Aircraft Apprentices Pipe Band and Trumpeters from Royal Air Force, Halton
The Band of the Army Apprentices School, Arborfield
Resident Bands: The Band of the Royal Army Service Corps
The Band of the Royal Air Force

The Royal Tournament 1948
Massed Bands from the Royal Naval School of Music
Staff Band of the Royal Naval School of Music
Resident Band: The Band of the Life Guards

The Royal Tournament 1949
Bands and Trumpeters of The Royal Naval School of Music
Corps of Drums of:
1st Bn. Welsh Guards
Guards Depot, Caterham
Pipes and Drums of:
1st Bn. Scots Guards
1st Bn. Irish Guards
Resident Band: The Band of the Royal Horse Guards (The Blues)

The Royal Tournament 1950
Massed Bands of the Royal Air Force
Central Band of the Royal Air Force
Regional Bands of the Royal Air Force
Central Band of the Women's Royal Air Force
Resident Band: The Band of the Life Guards

The Royal Tournament 1951
The Band and Trumpeters of the Royal Military School of Music, Kneller Hall
Massed Pipes and Drums
2nd Bn. Scots Guards
1st Bn. The Royal Scots (The Royal Regiment)
1st Bn. The Royal Scots Fusiliers
1st Bn. The Highland Light Infantry (City of Glasgow Regiment)
The Band of H.M. Royal Marines (Royal Marines School of Music)
Central Band of the Royal Air Force
Resident Band: The Band of the Royal Horse Guards (The Blues)

The Royal Tournament 1952
The Band and Trumpeters of the Royal Military School of Music, Kneller Hall
Band of the Royal Air Force Regiment
Resident Band: The Band of the Life Guards

The Royal Tournament 1953
The Massed Bands
4th/7th Royal Dragoon Guards

1st Bn. The Royal Berkshire Regiment (Princess Charlotte of Wales's)
Massed Bands of H.M. Royal Marines
No. 1 Regional Band, Royal Air Force
No. 2 Regional Band, Royal Air Force
Massed Pipes and Drums:
1st Bn. Royal Scots Fusiliers
2nd Bn. The Black Watch (Royal Highland Regiment)
1st Bn. Seaforth Highlanders (Ross-shire Buffs, The Duke of Albany's)
1st Canadian Highland Battalion
The Band of H.M. Royal Marines (Royal Marines School of Music)
The Staff Band of the Women's Royal Army Corps
The Central Band of the Women's Royal Air Force
Resident Band: The Band of the Life Guards

The Royal Tournament 1954
Massed Bands of H.M. Royal Marines
H.M. Royal Marines, Plymouth
H.M. Royal Marines (Royal Marines School of Music)
Massed Pipes and Drums of Scottish Regiments:
1st Bn. Scots Guards
1st Bn. The King's Own Scottish Borderers
1st Bn. The Cameronians (Scottish Rifles)
The Staff Band of the Women's Royal Army Corps
The Central Band of the Women's Royal Air Force
The Band of the Royal Air Force Regiment
Resident Band: The Band of the Royal Horse Guards (The Blues)

The Royal Tournament 1955
Massed Bands of the Royal Air Force
Central Band of the Royal Air Force
No. 1 Regional Band, Royal Air Force
No. 4 Regional Band, Royal Air Force
No. 5 Regional Band, Royal Air Force
Band of the Royal Air Force Regiment
Central Band of the Women's Royal Air Force
Pipe Band of the Pakistan Police
Massed Pipers and Drummers of the Arab Legion
Band and Drums of 1st Bn. The East Surrey Regiment
Resident Band: The Band of the Royal Army Service Corps

The Royal Tournament 1956
The Massed Bands and Bugles of the Light Infantry Brigade
1st Bn. The Somerset Light Infantry (Prince Albert's)
1st Bn. The Oxfordshire and Buckinghamshire Light Infantry
1st Bn. The King's Own Yorkshire Light Infantry
1st Bn. The Durham Light Infantry
The Drums of the Fort Henry Guard of Kingston, Ontario
The Band of the Federation of Malaya Police
Resident Band: The Band of 1st Bn. The Parachute Regiment

The Royal Tournament 1957
The Massed Bands of H.M. Royal Marines
H.M. Royal Marines, Portsmouth
H.M. Royal Marines, Plymouth
H.M. Royal Marines, H.M.S. Daedelus
H.M. Royal Marines (Royal Marines School of Music)
The Memorial Silver Trumpets of the Royal Marines School of Music
The Massed Drums, Pipes and Bugles of the North Irish Brigade
1st Bn. The Royal Inniskilling Fusiliers
1st Bn. The Royal Ulster Rifles
1st Bn. The Royal Irish Fusiliers (Princess Victoria's)
The Band of the Royal Air Force Regiment
The Band of the King's African Rifles - Tribal Display and Drill
Resident Band: The Rhine Staff Band of the Royal Tank Regiment

The Royal Tournament 1958
Massed Bands of the Royal Air Force
Central Band of the Royal Air Force
No. 1 Regional Band, Royal Air Force
No. 4 Regional Band, Royal Air Force
No. 5 Regional Band, Royal Air Force
Central Band of the Women's Royal Air Force
Massed Pipes and Drums of the Scottish Regiments
Scots Guards
1st Bn. The Royal Scots Fusiliers
1st Bn. Seaforth Highlanders (Ross-Shire Buffs, The Duke of Albany's)
Representatives of:
The King's Own Scottish Borderers
The Cameronians (Scottish Rifles)
The Brigade of Gurkhas
Resident Band: Band of the 7th Queen's Own Hussars

The Royal Tournament 1959
The Massed Bands:
The Royal Artillery Mounted Band
1st Bn. The South Wales Borderers (The 24th Regiment)
1st Bn. The Gloucestershire Regiment (28th/61st)
1st Bn. The Royal Sussex Regiment
1st Bn. The Royal Hampshire Regiment
The Staff Band of the Women's Royal Army Corps
Princess Patricia's Canadian Light Infantry
The Band of H.M. Royal Marines (Royal Marines School of Music)
The Staff Band of the Women's Royal Army Corps
The Central Band of the Women's Royal Air Force
Combined Women's Services Club Swinging Display
Resident Band: The Band of the Corps of Royal Engineers (Chatham)

The Royal Tournament 1960
Massed Bands of H.M. Royal Marines
H.M. Royal Marines, Commander-in-Chief, The Nore
H.M. Royal Marines, Flag Officer Air (Home)
H.M. Royal Marines, Britannia Royal Naval College
H.M. Royal Marines, H.M.S. Raleigh
H.M. Royal Marines, H.M.S. St. Vincent
H.M. Royal Marines, Portsmouth Group
H.M. Royal Marines (Royal Marines School of Music)
Massed Military Band and Pipe Bands of The Brigade of Gurkhas
Band and Drums of the Queen's Own Nigerian Regiment
Resident Band: Band of 1st Bn. The King's Own Royal Border Regiment

The Royal Tournament 1961
Massed Bands of the Royal Air Force
Resident Band: Band of 1st Bn. The King's Own Royal Border Regiment

The Royal Tournament 1962
Massed Bands of H.M. Royal Marines
H.M. Royal Marines, Flag Officer Air (Home)
H.M. Royal Marines, H.M.S. St. Vincent
H.M. Royal Marines, H.M.S. Raleigh
H.M. Royal Marines, Portsmouth Group
H.M. Royal Marines, Plymouth Group
H.M. Royal Marines (Royal Marines School of Music)
Massed Pipes and Drums of Scottish and Irish Regiments
1st Bn. Scots Guards
1st Bn. The Cameronians (Scottish Rifles)
1st Bn. The Royal Ulster Rifles
1st Bn. The Royal Irish Fusiliers (Princess Victoria's)
Massed Mounted Bands:
The Life Guards
The Royal Horse Guards (The Blues)
Resident Band: Band of 1st, The Queen's Dragoon Guards

The Royal Tournament 1963
The Massed Bands of the Royal Armoured Corps
5th Royal Inniskilling Dragoon Guards
The Royal Dragoons (1st Dragoons)
Royal Scots Greys (2nd Dragoons)
10th Royal Hussars (Prince of Wales's Own)
17th/21st Lancers
The Cambrai Staff Band of the Royal Tank Regiment
The Rhine Staff Band of the Royal Tank Regiment
The Band of H.M. Royal Marines, Plymouth Group
The Band of H.M. Royal Marines, Commander-in-Chief, Plymouth
The Fort Henry Guard of Kingston, Ontario
Resident Band: Band of the Royal Army Ordnance Corps

The Royal Tournament 1964
The Massed Bands of H.M. Royal Marines
H.M. Royal Marines, Plymouth Group
H.M. Royal Marines, Commander-in-Chief, Portsmouth
H.M. Royal Marines, Commander-in-Chief, Plymouth
H.M. Royal Marines, Commander-in-Chief, Home Fleet
H.M. Royal Marines, Flag Officer Naval Air Command
H.M. Royal Marines, H.M.S. Condor
H.M. Royal Marines, H.M.S. Raleigh
H.M. Royal Marines, H.M.S. Thunderer
H.M. Royal Marines (Royal Marines School of Music)
The Massed Bands, Pipes and Drums of the North Irish Brigade
1st Bn. The Royal Inniskilling Fusiliers
1st Bn. The Royal Ulster Rifles
1st Bn. The Royal Irish Fusiliers (Princess Victoria's)
Resident Band: Band of the Royal Corps of Signals

The Royal Tournament 1965
The Massed Bands of the Royal Air Force
Band and Bugles of the 2nd King Edward VII's Own Gurkha Rifles (The Sirmoor Rifles)
Representative Pipes and Drums of The Brigade of Gurkhas
The Band of the Fiji Military Forces
Band and Drums of the Junior Guardsmen's Company
Resident Band: The Staff Band of the Royal Army Medical Corps

The Royal Tournament 1966
The Massed Bands of the Royal Artillery
The Royal Artillery (Woolwich) Band
The Royal Artillery Mounted Band
The Royal Artillery (BAOR) Band
The Junior Musicians Troop, Royal Artillery
The Band of the Junior Leaders Regiment, Royal Artillery
The Massed Bands and Bugles of the Light Infantry Brigade
Band of 1st Bn. The Somerset and Cornwall Light Infantry
Band and Bugles of:
1st Bn. The King's Own Yorkshire Light Infantry
1st Bn. The King's Shropshire Light Infantry
1st Bn. The Durham Light Infantry
The Band of H.M. Royal Marines, Plymouth Group
Pipes and Drums of the Pakistan Frontier Constabulary
Resident Band: Staff Band of the Corps of Royal Electrical and Mechanical Engineers

The Royal Tournament 1967
The Massed Bands of the Royal Air Force
The Massed Pipes and Drums of the Lowland and Highland Brigades
1st Bn. The Royal Scots (The Royal Regiment)
1st Bn. The Royal Highland Fusiliers (Princess Margaret's Own Glasgow and Ayrshire Regiment)
1st Bn. The King's Own Scottish Borderers

1st Bn. The Cameronians (Scottish Rifles)
1st Bn. The Black Watch (Royal Highland Regiment)
1st Bn. Queen's Own Highlanders (Seaforth and Camerons)
1st Bn. The Gordon Highlanders
Band of H.M. Royal Marines, Portsmouth Group
The Band, Drums and Dancers of the Jamaica Regiment
Resident Band: The Alamein Staff Band of the Royal Tank Regiment

The Royal Tournament 1968
The Massed Bands of H.M. Royal Marines
H.M. Royal Marines, Portsmouth Group
H.M. Royal Marines, Plymouth Group
H.M. Royal Marines (Royal Marines School of Music)
The Royal Marines Symphony Orchestra
The Royal Marines Oceanaires Dance Orchestra
Regimental Band and Bugles of 2nd King Edward VII's Own Gurkha Rifles (The Sirmoor Rifles)
Representative Pipes and Drums of the Brigade of Gurkhas
Corps of Drums and Drill Team of 2nd Bn. Princess Patricia's Canadian Light Infantry
Resident Band: Band of the Corps of Royal Engineers (Aldershot)

The Royal Tournament 1969
The Massed Bands of the Royal Armoured Corps
5th Royal Inniskilling Dragoon Guards
The Royal Scots Greys (2nd Dragoons)
The Queen's Own Hussars
The Queen's Royal Irish Hussars
9th/12th Royal Lancers (Prince of Wales's)
14th/20th King's Hussars
The Rhine Staff Band of the Royal Tank Regiment
Fanfara of the 3rd Bersagleri Regiment
Resident Band: The Midland Band of the Royal Air Force

The Royal Tournament 1970
The Massed Bands of the Royal Air Force
Central Band of the Royal Air Force
Western Band of the Royal Air Force
Midland Band of the Royal Air Force
Band of the Royal Air Force Regiment
Central Band of the Women's Royal Air Force
Massed Bands and Bugles of the Light Division
Band of 2nd Bn. The Light Infantry
Band and Bugles of:
3rd Bn. The Light Infantry
1st Bn. The Royal Green Jackets
3rd Bn. The Royal Green Jackets
Band of the Royal Brunei Malay Regiment
Resident Band: Band of the Royal Corps of Signals

The Royal Tournament 1971
The Massed Bands of H.M. Royal Marines
H.M. Royal Marines, Portsmouth
H.M. Royal Marines, Plymouth
H.M. Royal Marines (Royal Marines School of Music)
The Massed Pipes and Drums of the Scottish Division
1st Bn. The Royal Scots (The Royal Regiment)
1st Bn. The King's Own Scottish Borderers
1st Bn. Queen's Own Highlanders (Seaforth and Camerons)
1st Bn. The Gordon Highlanders
Balaklava Company, Argyll and Sutherland Highlanders (Princess Louise's)
The Band of the Brigade of Gurkhas (2nd King Edward VII's Own Gurkha Rifles)
Bugles of 2nd King Edward VII's Own Gurkha Rifles (The Sirmoor Rifles)
Resident Band: Staff Band of the Royal Army Medical Corps

The Royal Tournament 1972
Massed Bands and Drums of the Infantry
2nd Bn. The Royal Regiment of Fusiliers
3rd Bn. The Royal Regiment of Fusiliers
1st Bn. The King's Regiment
1st Bn. The Devonshire and Dorset Regiment
1st Bn. The Duke of Wellington's Regiment (West Riding)
Corps of Drums:
2nd Bn. The Royal Regiment of Fusiliers
3rd Bn. The Royal Regiment of Fusiliers
1st Bn. The Devonshire and Dorset Regiment
Singapore Armed Forces
Southern Band of the Royal Air Force
Resident Band: Staff Band of the Corps of Royal Electrical and Mechanical Engineers

The Royal Tournament 1973
The Massed Bands of the Royal Air Force
Central Band of the Royal Air Force
Western Band of the Royal Air Force
Southern Band of the Royal Air Force
Band of the Royal Air Force Regiment
The Bands, Pipes, Bugles, Drums and Dancers of:
1st Bn. The Royal Irish Rangers
2nd Bn. The Royal Irish Rangers
(Also provided the Resident Band)
The Band of the Royal Barbados Police
The Charanga of the Portugese Republican National Guard

The Royal Tournament 1974
The Massed Bands of H.M. Royal Marines
H.M. Royal Marines, Commander-in-Chief, Naval Home Command
H.M. Royal Marines, Commando Forces
H.M. Royal Marines, Commando Training Centre
H.M. Royal Marines, Britannia Royal Naval College
H.M. Royal Marines, H.M.S. Ganges
H.M. Royal Marines (Royal Marines School of Music)
Southern Band of the Royal Air Force
Drummers and Dancers of the Sri Lanka Police Reserve
Resident Band: Staff Band of the Royal Army Ordnance Corps

The Royal Tournament 1975
The Massed Bands of the Royal Armoured Corps
Royal Scots Dragoon Guards (Carabiniers and Greys)
4th/7th Royal Dragoon Guards
The Queen's Own Hussars
The Royal Hussars (Prince of Wales's Own)
13th/18th Royal Hussars (Queen Mary's Own)
14th/20th King's Hussars
16th/5th The Queen's Royal Lancers
The Cambrai Staff Band of the Royal Tank Regiment
The Pipes and Drums of The Royal Scots Dragoon Guards (Carabiniers and Greys)
The Marine Band of the Royal Netherlands Navy
Pipes and Drums of the Royal Netherlands Marine Corps
The Pipes and Drums of the Australian State Police Forces
Resident Band: The Royal Artillery Band

The Royal Tournament 1976
The Massed Bands of the Royal Air Force
Central Band of the Royal Air Force
Western Band of the Royal Air Force
Southern Band of the Royal Air Force
Band of the Royal Air Force Regiment
Pipes of the Kuwait Army
Resident Band: Band of the Royal Corps of Signals

The Royal Tournament 1977
The Massed Bands of H.M. Royal Marines
H.M. Royal Marines, Commander-in-Chief, Naval Home Command
H.M. Royal Marines, Commander-in-Chief, Fleet
H.M. Royal Marines, Flag Officer Scotland and Northern Ireland
H.M. Royal Marines, Flag Officer Naval Air Command
H.M. Royal Marines (Royal Marines School of Music)
The Band of the Australian Army Band Corps
The British Columbia Beefeaters Band
Resident Band: Band of the Corps of Royal Engineers (Chatham)

The Royal Tournament 1978
Massed Bands of the Infantry
Composite Band from the Guards Division
3rd Bn. The Royal Anglian Regiment
1st Bn. The Royal Irish Rangers
2nd Bn. The Royal Irish Rangers
1st Bn. The Duke of Edinburgh's Royal Regiment (Berkshire and Wiltshire)
1st Bn. The Light Infantry
1st Bn. The Parachute Regiment
Pipes and Drums:
1st Bn. Irish Guards
1st Bn. Royal Irish Rangers
2nd Bn. The Royal Irish Rangers
Bugles:
1st Bn. The Royal Irish Rangers
2nd Bn. The Royal Irish Rangers
The Bands of the Royal Hong Kong Police
The Pipes, Drums and Bugles of 6th Queen Elizabeth's Own Gurkha Rifles
Resident Band: Staff Band of the Royal Army Medical Corps

The Royal Tournament 1979
The Massed Bands of the Royal Air Force
Central Band of the Royal Air Force
Band of the Royal Air Force College
Western Band of the Royal Air Force
Band of the Royal Air Force Regiment
The Florida Suncoast Sound of Gold
Resident Band: Staff Band of the Women's Royal Army Corps

The Royal Tournament 1980
The Massed Bands of the Three Services
The Band of the Irish Guards
Pipes and Drums, 1st Bn. Irish Guards
H.M. Royal Marines (Royal Marines School of Music)
Central Band of the Royal Air Force
The Kenya Army Band
Resident Band: Staff Band of the Corps of Royal Electrical and Mechanical Engineers

The Royal Tournament 1981
The Massed Bands of H.M. Royal Marines
H.M. Royal Marines, Flag Officer Plymouth
H.M. Royal Marines, Flag Officer Scotland and Northern Ireland
H.M. Royal Marines, Flag Officer Naval Air Command
H.M. Royal Marines, Commando Forces
H.M. Royal Marines, Commando Training Centre
H.M. Royal Marines (Royal Marines School of Music)
The Band of the Royal Air Force Regiment
The Marine Band of the Royal Netherlands Navy
The Pipes and Drums and the Steel Band of the
Royal Netherlands Marine Corps
Resident Band: Band of the Royal Corps of Signals

The Royal Tournament 1982
The Massed Bands
1st The Queen's Dragoon Guards
The Royal Scots Dragoon Guards (Carabiniers and Greys)
The Queen's Own Hussars
The Queen's Royal Irish Hussars
The Royal Hussars (Prince of Wales's Own)

14th/20th King's Hussars
15th/19th The King's Royal Hussars
Corps of Royal Engineers (Aldershot)
Royal Army Medical Corps
Royal Army Ordnance Corps
Corps of Royal Electrical and Mechanical Engineers
Dismounted Trumpeters and 18th Century Band found from:
The Band of the Blues and Royals (Royal Horse Guards & 1st Dragoons) (first week) and The Band of the Life Guards (second and third weeks)
State Trumpeters and Drum Horses of the Household Cavalry
Mounted Trumpeters and Drum Horse of the
Royal Scots Dragoon Guards (Carabiniers and Greys)
Drum Horse of the Queen's Own Hussars
Pipers from:
The Guards Depot Piping School
G (London Scottish) Company, 1st Bn. 51st Highland Volunteers
Choir from The Guards Depot
Resident Band: Staff Band of the Women's Royal Army Corps

The Royal Tournament 1983

The Massed Bands of the Royal Air Force
Central Band of the Royal Air Force
Band of the Royal Air Force College
Western Band of the Royal Air Force
Band of the Royal Air Force Regiment
Massed Pipes and Drums
The Royal Scots Dragoon Guards (Carabiniers and Greys)
4th Royal Tank Regiment
2nd Bn. Scots Guards
1st Bn. King's Own Scottish Borderers
1st Bn. The Gordon Highlanders
1st Bn. 51st Highland Volunteers
Resident Band: The Royal Artillery Band

The Royal Tournament 1984

The Massed Bands of H.M. Royal Marines
H.M. Royal Marines, Commander-in-Chief, Naval Home Command
H.M. Royal Marines, Commander-in-Chief, Fleet
H.M. Royal Marines, Flag Officer Scotland and Northern Ireland
H.M. Royal Marines, Commando Forces
H.M. Royal Marines, Commando Training Centre
H.M. Royal Marines (Royal Marines School of Music)
The Orchestra of H.M. Royal Marines
Resident Band: Band of 1st Bn. The Royal Green Jackets

The Royal Tournament 1985

The Massed Bands
4th/7th Royal Dragoon Guards
The Queen's Own Hussars
The Queen's Royal Irish Hussars
Grenadier Guards
1st Bn. The Royal Anglian Regiment (Norfolk, Suffolk and Cambridgeshire)
3rd Bn. The Royal Anglian Regiment (Bedfordshire, Hertfordshire and Essex)
1st Bn. The Devonshire and Dorset Regiment
Corps of Drums:
3rd Bn. The Royal Anglian Regiment (Bedfordshire, Hertfordshire and Essex)
1st Bn. The Devonshire and Dorset Regiment
State Trumpeters and Drum Horses of the Household Cavalry
Drum Horse of the Queen's Own Hussars
Massed Bands and Bugles of the Light Division
The Light Infantry Corunna Band
The Light Infantry Salamanca Band
The Normandy Band, The Royal Green Jackets
The Peninsular Band, The Royal Green Jackets
Bugles:
3rd Bn. The Light Infantry
6th Bn. The Light Infantry

7th Bn. The Light Infantry
1st Bn. The Royal Green Jackets
2nd Bn. The Royal Green Jackets
3rd Bn. The Royal Green Jackets
The Band of the Royal Air Force Regiment
The Band, Pipes and Drums of the Jordan Armed Forces
Resident Band: Band of 2nd Bn. The Royal Anglian Regiment (Lincolnshire, Leicestershire and Northamptonshire)

The Royal Tournament 1986
The Massed Bands of the Royal Air Force
Central Band of the Royal Air Force
Band of the Royal Air Force College
Western Band of the Royal Air Force
Band of the Royal Air Force Regiment
Pipes and Drums of the Royal Air Force
The Band of the Brigade of Gurkhas (2nd King Edward VII's Own Gurkha Rifles)
Bugles of 2nd King Edward VII's Own Gurkha Rifles (The Sirmoor Rifles)
The Band of the Papua New Guinea Constabulary
The Charanga of the Portugese Republican Guard
Resident Band: Staff Band of the Women's Royal Army Corps

The Royal Tournament 1987
The Massed Bands of H.M. Royal Marines
H.M. Royal Marines, Commander-in-Chief, Naval Home Command
H.M. Royal Marines, Commander-in-Chief, Fleet
H.M. Royal Marines, Commando Forces
H.M. Royal Marines (Royal Marines School of Music)
The Dance Band of H.M. Royal Marines
The Massed Bands of the Australian Defence Force
The Band of the Royal Australian Navy
The Band of the Royal Military College, Duntroon
The Royal Australian Air Force Central Band
Resident Band: Band of the Corps of Royal Engineers

The Royal Tournament 1988
Mounted Band of the Blues and Royals (Royal Horse Guards & 1st Dragoons)
The Massed Bands
Band of the Welsh Guards
The Quebec Band, The Queen's Regiment
1st Bn. The King's Own Royal Border Regiment
Duke of Kent's Band, The Royal Regiment of Fusiliers
St. George's Band, The Royal Regiment of Fusiliers
1st Bn. The Devonshire and Dorset Regiment
1st Bn. The Prince of Wales's Own Regiment of Yorkshire
1st Bn. The Green Howards (Alexandra, Princess of Wales's Own Yorkshire Regiment)
1st Bn. The 22nd (Cheshire) Regiment
1st Bn. The Royal Welch Fusiliers
1st Bn. The Royal Regiment of Wales (24th/41st Foot)
1st Bn. The Gloucestershire Regiment
1st Bn. The Worcestershire and Sherwood Foresters Regiment (29th/45th Foot)
1st Bn. The Duke of Wellington's Regiment (West Riding)
1st Bn. The Royal Hampshire Regiment
Corps of Drums:
The Queen's Regiment
1st Bn. The King's Own Royal Border Regiment
1st Bn. The Royal Regiment of Fusiliers
2nd Bn. The Royal Regiment of Fusiliers
1st Bn. The Devonshire and Dorset Regiment

1st Bn. The Prince of Wales's Own Regiment of Yorkshire
1st Bn. The 22nd (Cheshire) Regiment
1st Bn. The Royal Regiment of Wales (24th/41st Foot)
1st Bn. the Worcestershire and Sherwood Foresters Regiment (29th/45th Foot)
1st Bn. The Royal Hampshire Regiment
Corps of Drums of H.M. Royal Marines
Drummers of the Dutch Grenadiers
Resident Band: 2nd Royal Tank Regiment

The Royal Tournament 1989
The Massed Bands of the Royal Air Force
Central Band of the Royal Air Force
Band of the Royal Air Force College
Western Band of the Royal Air Force
Band of the Royal Air Force Regiment
The Royal Air Force Squadronaires
The Massed Bands of NATO
The Canadian Forces Schol of Music
Slevigshe Fodregiment's Musik Korps (Denmark)
Heeres Musik Korps 1, Hanover (Germany)
Fanfare Dei Bersaglieri (Italy)
Interservice Bands of The Netherlands
Royal Guard Band (Spain)
126th Army Band (Mitchigan National Guard) (USA)
and Bands from Belgium, Portugal and Turkey
The Band of the Warsaw District, Poland
The Pomeranian Military District Band, Poland
Resident Band: Staff Band of the Royal Army Ordnance Corps

The Royal Tournament 1990
The Massed Bands of H.M. Royal Marines
H.M. Royal Marines, Commander-in-Chief, Naval Home Command
H.M. Royal Marines, Commander-in-Chief, Fleet
H.M. Royal Marines, Flag Officer Plymouth
H.M. Royal Marines, Flag Officer Scotland and Northern Ireland
H.M. Royal Marines, Commandos
H.M. Royal Marines (Royal Marines School of Music)
The Royal Netherlands Marine Corps
The Spanish Marine Corps
The United States Marine Corps, 2nd Marine Division Band
Resident Band: Staff Band of the Women's Royal Army Corps

The Royal Tournament 1991
The Massed Bands of the Cavalry and Royal Tank Regiment
Mounted Band of the Blues and Royals (Royal Horse Guards & 1st Dragoons)
1st, The Queen's Dragoon Guards
The Royal Scots Dragoon Guards (Carabiniers and Greys)
4th/7th Royal Dragoon Guards
5th Royal Inniskilling Dragoon Guards
The Queen's Own Hussars
The Queen's Royal Irish Hussars
9th/12th Royal Lancers (Prince of Wales's)
The Royal Hussars (Prince of Wales's Own)
13th/18th Royal Hussars (Queen Mary's Own)
14th/20th King's Hussars
15th/19th, The King's Royal Hussars
16th/5th, The Queen's Royal Lancers
17th/21st Lancers
1st Royal Tank Regiment
2nd Royal Tank Regiment
Massed Pipes and Drums
The Royal Scots Dragoon Guards (Carabiniers and Greys)
1st Bn. Scots Guards
The Royal Irish Rangers (27th (Inniskilling), 83rd and 87th)
Composite Pipes and Drums from The Brigade of Gurkhas
Resident Band: Band of the Royal Corps of Signals

The Royal Tournament 1992
The Massed Bands of the Royal Air Force
Central Band of the Royal Air Force
Band of the Royal Air Force, Germany
Band of the Royal Air Force College
Western Band of the Royal Air Force
Band of the Royal Air Force Regiment
The Conqueror Band from Los Altos High School, California
Resident Band: Staff Band of the Corps of Royal Electrical and Mechanical Engineers

The Royal Tournament 1993
The Massed Bands of H.M. Royal Marines
H.M. Royal Marines, Commander-in-Chief, Naval Home Command
H.M. Royal Marines, Commander-in-Chief, Fleet
H.M. Royal Marines, Flag Officer Plymouth
H.M. Royal Marines, Flag Officer Scotland and Northern Ireland
H.M. Royal Marines, Britannia Royal Naval College
H.M. Royal Marines (Royal Marines School of Music)
The Russian Navy Band
Resident Band: The Royal Artillery Band

The Royal Tournament 1994
The Massed Bands of the Household Division
Mounted Band of The Life Guards
Band of the Grenadier Guards
Band of the Coldstream Guards
Band of the Irish Guards
Band of the Welsh Guards
The Massed Bands and Bugles of the Light Division
The Light Infantry Corunna Band
The Light Infantry Salamanca Band
The Normandy Band, The Royal Green Jackets
The Peninsular Band, The Royal Green Jackets
Bugles from The Light Infantry and The Royal Green Jackets
Band of the Brigade of Gurkhas
Pipes and Drums from The Brigade of Gurkhas
Trumpeters of the Royal Military School of Music, Kneller Hall
Massed Drummers of NATO
Resident Band: Band of the Adjutant General's Corps

The Royal Tournament 1995
The Massed Bands of the Royal Air Force
Central Band of the Royal Air Force
Band of the Royal Air Force College
Western Band of the Royal Air Force
Band of the Royal Air Force Regiment
Royal Air Force Squadronaires
Massed Bands of the Commonwealth Air Forces
The Royal Australian Air Force Central Band
The Canadian Forces Air Command Band
The Indian Air Force
The Central Army Band of the Russian Federation
The U.S. Army Band, Europe
The French Foreign Legion
Resident Band: Band of the Army Air Corps

The Royal Tournament 1996
The Massed Bands of H.M. Royal Marines
H.M. Royal Marines, Portsmouth
H.M. Royal Marines, Plymouth
H.M. Royal Marines, Scotland
H.M. Royal Marines, Commando Training Centre
Pipes and Drums of the The Queen's Royal Hussars (Queen's Own and Royal Irish)
Pipes and Drums of 1st Bn. Irish Guards
Band, Bugles, Pipes and Drums of The Royal Irish Regiment (27th (Inniskilling), 83rd & 87th and Ulster Defence Regiment)

Band of the Royal Ulster Constabulary
Irish Traditional Youth Bands from Dublin and Cork
The Band, Pipes and Drums of the Royal Hong Kong Police
Resident Band: Band of the Parachute Regiment

The Royal Tournament 1997

The Massed Bands of the Household Division
Mounted Band of The Blues and Royals (Royal Horse Guards & 1st Dragoons)
Band of the Grenadier Guards
Band of the Scots Guards
Band of the Irish Guards
Band of the Welsh Guards
The New Zealand Defence Force Maori Culture Group
Resident Band: Band of the Hussars and Light Dragoons

The Royal Tournament 1998

The Massed Bands of the Royal Air Force
Central Band of the Royal Air Force
Western Band of the Royal Air Force
Band of the Royal Air Force Regiment
Pipers of the Royal Air Force
The Band of the South Australia Police
Resident Band: The King's Division Waterloo Band

The Royal Tournament 1999

Massed Bands of the Three Services
Mounted Band of The Blues and Royals (Royal Horse Guards & 1st Dragoons)
Band of the Grenadier Guards
Band of the Coldstream Guards
H.M. Royal Marines, Plymouth
H.M. Royal Marines, Commando Training Centre

APPENDIX E – FIELD GUN RESULTS

Year	Inter-Command Challenge Cup	Points	Aggregate Time Cup	Fastest Time Cup	Least Penalty Points	Copenhagen Cup
1907	H.M.S. Cambridge					
1908	H.M.S. Victory					
1909	H.M.S. Excellent					
1910	H.M.S. Pembroke 'B'					
1911	H.M.S. Victory					
1912	H.M.S. Excellent					
1913	Portsmouth					
1914	H.M.S. Pembroke					
	1915 – 1918 No Competition					
1919	Portsmouth					
1920	Portsmouth					
1921	Portsmouth					
1922	Portsmouth					
1923	Devonport					
1924	H.M.S. Pembroke		Pem A	Pem A		
1925	Portsmouth		Pem A	RM A		
1926	Devonport		Exc	Viv B		
1927	Devonport		Viv A	Viv A		
1928	H.M.S. Pembroke		Pem B	Pem B		
1929	H.M.S. Pembroke		Pem B	Pem		
1930	Not Awarded		Viv	Pem		
1931	Not Awarded		Pem	Exc		
1932	Not Awarded		Pem	Pem		
1933	Not Awarded		Pem	Pem		
1934	Not Awarded		Pem	Pem		
1935	Not Awarded		Chat	Dev		
1936	No Competition					
1937	R.N.B. Chatham		Chat S	Chat S		
1938	Devonport					
1939	Devonport					
	1940 – 1946 No Competition					

Year	Inter-Command Challenge Cup	Points	Aggregate Time Cup	Fastest Time Cup	Least Penalty Points	Copenhagen Cup
	1947 – 1960 12 Competition Runs per Crew (Max 24 Points)					
1947	Devonport	22	Air	Air		
1948	Portsmouth	21	Port	Port		
1949	Portsmouth	23	Port	Air		
1950	Fleet Air Arm	22	Air	Air		
1951	Devonport	19	Dev	Chat		
1952	Devonport	22	Dev	Dev		
1953	Devonport	24	Dev	Dev		
1954	Devonport	20	Dev	Dev		
1955	Portsmouth/Devonport	21	Dev	Dev		
1956	Fleet Air Arm	21	Air	Air		
1957	Portsmouth	19	Port	Port		
1958	Devonport	22	Dev	Dev		
1959	F.A.A./Devonport	21	Dev	Air		
1960	Fleet Air Arm	22	Air	Air		
	1961 – 1993 16 Competition Runs per Crew (Max 32 Points)					
1961	Fleet Air Arm	23	Air	Port/Air		
1962	Fleet Air Arm	28	Dev	Air		
1963	Devonport	26	Dev	Air		
1964	Fleet Air Arm	30	Air	Air		
1965	F.A.A./Devonport		Air	Dev		
1966	Fleet Air Arm	32	Air	Air		
1967	Fleet Air Arm	26	Air	Dev		Air
1968	Fleet Air Arm	30	Air	Air		Air
1969	Fleet Air Arm	28	Air	Air		Air
1970	Portsmouth	27	Port	Port		Dev
1971	Fleet Air Arm	27	Air	Air		Port
1972	Portsmouth/F.A.A.	27	Air	Air		
1973	Fleet Air Arm	28	Air	Port		
1974	Fleet Air Arm	28	Air	Port		Port
1975	Portsmouth	27	Port	Port		Port
1976	Fleet Air Arm	29	Air	Port/Air		Air
1977	Devonport	27	Dev	Dev	Dev	Dev
1978	Portsmouth/Devonport	26	Dev	Dev	Air	Port

Year	Inter-Command Challenge Cup	Points	Aggregate Time Cup	Fastest Time Cup	Least Penalty Points	Copenhagen Cup
1979	Fleet Air Arm	25	Air	Air	Air	Port
1980	Devonport	26	Port	Dev	Port	Port
1981	Portsmouth	28	Port	Port	Air	Port
1982	Fleet Air Arm	30	Air	Air	Port	Air
1983	Devonport	31	Dev	Dev	Dev	Port
1984	Portsmouth/F.A.A.	26	Port	Port	Port	Air
1985	Devonport	26	Dev	Air	Dev	Dev
1986	Portsmouth	26	Port	Port	Port	Port
1987	Portsmouth	27	Port	Port	Air	Air
1988	Fleet Air Arm	28	Dev	Air	Dev	Dev
1989	Devonport	25	Air	Air	Air	Port
1990	Fleet Air Arm	29	Air	Air	Air	Air
1991	Fleet Air Arm	30	Air	Air	Dev	Air
1992	Fleet Air Arm	30	Air	Air	Port	Air
1993	Devonport	22	Dev	Dev	Port	Air
	1994 – 1998 14 Competition Runs per Crew (Max 28 Points)					
1994	Devonport	26	Dev	Port	Dev	Dev
1995	Fleet Air Arm	22	Air	Air	Dev	Air
1996	Devonport	22	Dev	Air	Port	Port
1997	Portsmouth	25	Port	Port	Air	Port
1998	Devonport	23	Dev	Dev	Dev	Port
	1999 16 Competition Runs per Crew (Max 32 Points)					
1999	Devonport	29	Dev	Dev	Air	Air

With thanks to Devonport, Fleet Air Arm, and Portsmouth Field Gun Associations for providing the competition results and records.

Published Course Record Times

Year	Crew	Time
1935	Devonport	3.54.4
1937	Chatham	3.53.0
1938	Devonport Stokers	3.48.0
1949	Fleet Air Arm	3.38.6
1952	Devonport	3.33.8
1953	Devonport	3.21.8
1957	Portsmouth	3.11.6
1960	Fleet Air Arm	3.04.2
1961	Fleet Air Arm/Portsmouth	3.01.8
1962	Fleet Air Arm	2.54.0
1964	Fleet Air Arm	2.52.6
1965	Devonport	2.51.6
1966	Fleet Air Arm	2.50.8
1969	Fleet Air Arm	2.50.5
1971	Fleet Air Arm	2.48.0
1972	Fleet Air Arm	2.44.8
1973	Portsmouth	2.44.7
1978	Portsmouth	2.44.6
1979	Fleet Air Arm	2.44.4
1981	Portsmouth	2.42.4
1984	Portsmouth	2.40.6
1999	Devonport	2.40.43

APPENDIX F – EVOLUTION OF FIELD GUN

The first Field Gun Competition was staged at the Royal Naval & Military Tournament at Olympia in 1907, it remained a firm favourite with Tournament audiences up to the Last Run in 1999. The nature of the competition remained almost the same from 1950 onwards when the Tournament moved to Earls Court. However, the track used at Olympia evolved over time. The evolution is documented here, based the current information available from programme notes, photographs, newspaper reports, and diagrams. With thanks to the various members of the Field Gun Crews who provided information for this appendix.

Six crews took part in the first competition, one from the Naval Barracks and one from the Gunnery Schools from Portsmouth, Devonport, and Nore (Chatham). Two crews competed at each afternoon performance in 1907. Each crew was made up of 18 men. The programme notes state that the competition was staged on the "American System, All against All" so over the course of the Tournament each crew competed against all of the others once.

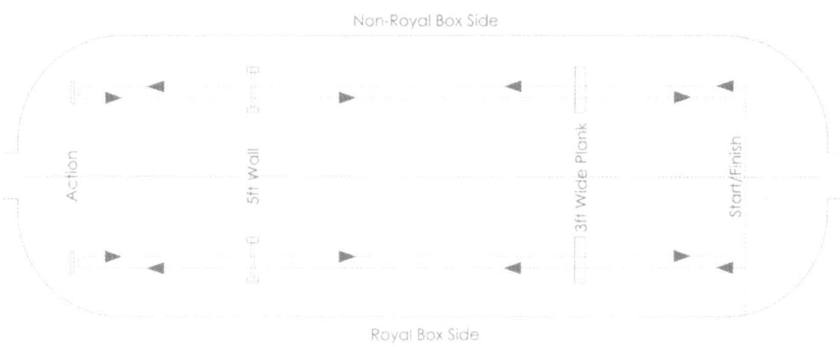

60 - Field Gun Competition layout 1907

The competing crews formed up at the Kensington (Olympia) Station[30] end of the arena. When given the signal to start, they set off down the arena. The first obstacle encountered by each crew was a set of planks (3 ft wide) at a height of 18 inches off the ground, the gun, limber, and crew had to pass underneath.

[30] The station was known as Addison Road until 1946, when it was renamed Kensington (Olympia).

They continued down the arena to the next obstacle, a 5ft high wall, which the crew, gun, and limber passed over. Each gun was brought into action, the programme notes say that "the muzzle being passed through a hole in a board before firing". The crews then returned to the start/finish line passing over and under the obstacles as before. The first crew to cross the line (providing that no rules had been broken) was awarded one point.

Following the first competition, the course was amended in 1908. The plank obstacle was replaced with the first chasm. The programme notes state that the chasm was formed from two ramps, 4ft high with a 2ft wide "flat top" on each side of the chasm. The ramps were set at an angle of 30 degrees (contemporary images appear to show ridges on the ramps although this is not mentioned in the programme). The chasm was set at 7ft 6in wide, a distance "governed by what is an easy jump for an ordinary man" according to the programme. It also stated that "no appliances are allowed to assist in crossing the obstacle".

The crews formed up at the end of the arena and set off as a staring pistol was fired. They raced down the arena to the chasm. The gun and limber were taken over by the crews "in any manner they please", the notes state that none of the kit or crew could be recovered if they fell in the chasm.

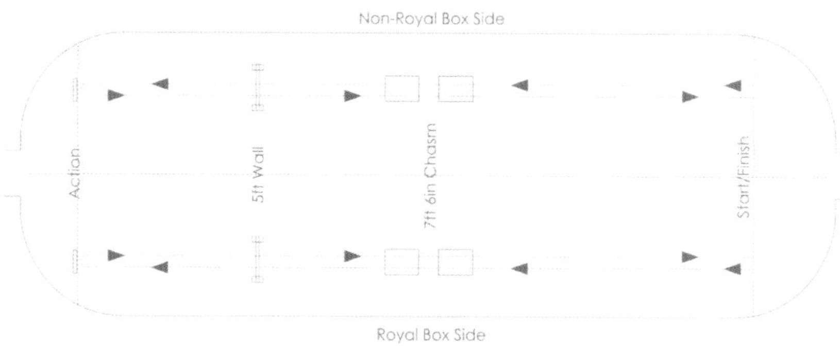

61 - Field Gun Competition layout 1908

The gun and limber were hooked up on the opposite side of the chasm and were pulled towards the 5 ft wall. The gun, limber, and crew passed over the wall and "advanced to cover, brought into action, and fired". The crews then returned over the same obstacles to the start line. The time stopped as the axle of the gun crossed the line (a pistol was fired to denote the finish).

The course was amended again in 1909, becoming a continuous loop. The start/finish line was moved to the the centre of the arena in line with the Royal Box. The crew running on the Royal Box Side took a clockwise route and the Non-Royal Box Side took an anti-clockwise route. The first part of the course was a sprint to the end of the arena before turning towards the audience around a post. The crews then took on the 7ft 6in chasm and 5 ft wall as they had done the previous year.

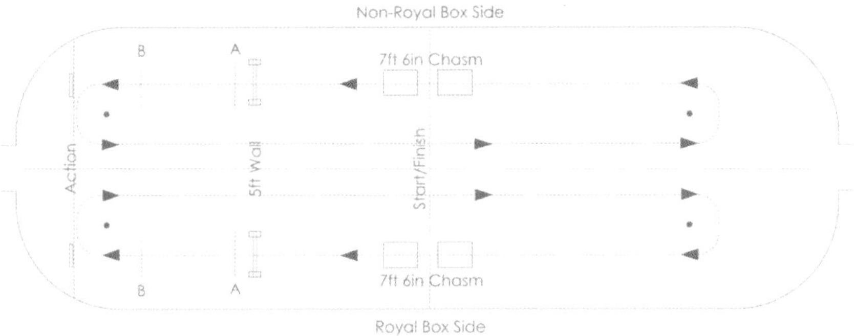

62 - Field Gun Competition layout 1909

After completing the wall, the programme notes state "the gun carriage is supposed to be disabled, and the gun, carriage, and wheels move off on top of the limber" at point A on the diagram. The gun is remounted onto the carriage and wheels at point B and is then brought into action, firing from a position of cover (through a hole in a board). The gun and limber was then pulled to the start/finish line in front of the Royal Box. Time penalties were awarded for "loss of gear or disobedience of rules", the crew which completed the course in the fastest time (including any penalties) was awarded the points for the run.

The course changed again 1912. The chasm was removed and replaced with a single ramp. The crews negotiated the ramp in both directions, up the sloped face on the run out and down the sloped face on the return leg. The rest of the course remained the same.

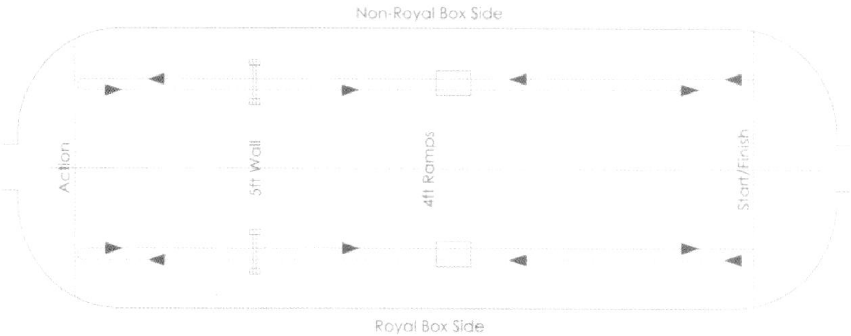

63 - Field Gun Competition layout 1912

Further amendments to the course came the following year. The 1914 programme notes describe the competing crews making "a raid into hostile territory on the far side of a river over a series of obstacles. These consist of two walls on either side of the river, which is 30ft wide". On the outward journey, the crews took their guns and limbers over the walls and on the return journey through a "narrow breach" in the walls. All the necessary spars and ropes were provided for the crews. On the return journey, all the equipment had to be unrigged and hauled out of reach of the enemy after recrossing the river.

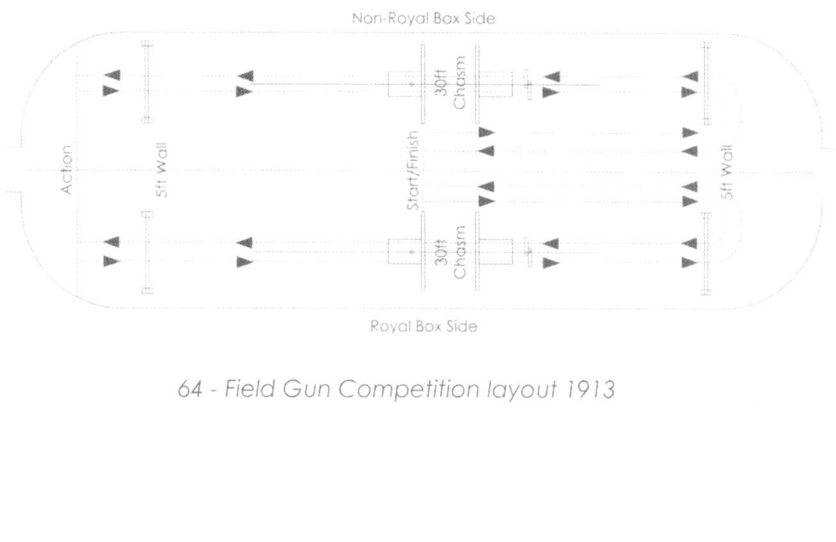

64 - Field Gun Competition layout 1913

The 1919 programme lists four teams with two crews each.

Portsmouth	H.M.S. Excellent (School of Gunnery)	H.M.S. Victory (R.N. Barracks)
Chatham	Two crews from H.M.S. Pembroke (R.N. Barracks)	
Devonport	Two crews from H.M.S. Vivid (R.N. Barracks)	
Royal Marines	Royal Marine Artillery (Eastney Barracks)	Royal Marine Light Infantry (Forton Barracks)

The 1923 programme provided more detail on the course. "Owing to the limited space in the arena, the crews have to start and finish their run down the centre of the course. In order to allow for this the gates between the home wall are swung open to let the gun through, and some of the ramps have to be removed after the river is crossed on the home run so that the finish may take place opposite the Royal Box".

The two crews started the race side by side in the centre of the arena, heading down the arena and turning outwards. They passed over the home wall and made their way to the 30 ft chasm, crossing it using the equipment provided. They then reassembled the gun and limber before passing over the second wall and bringing the gun into action, firing three rounds.

On the return, the crew, gun, and limber passed through holes in the walls. They crossed the chasm again, unrigging and bringing the equipment with them. The run was completed when the gun, or the last man from the crew crossed the line in front of the Royal Box.

When the Tournament returned after the Great War, the same format was used for the 1919 Field Gun Competition into the 1920s. However, in 1925 the number of obstacles was reduced to a single wall. The description of the course in the programme says that the crews crossed over the 5 ft wall enroute to engage the enemy at the far end of the arena.

After crossing over the wall "shortly before reaching the Action position, an enemy shell causes damage to both gun wheels, necessitating their exchange with those on the limber". This is similar to the "Brickwoods" Field

Gun Competition format, when both the Gun and Limber are held in the air while the wheels are exchanged.

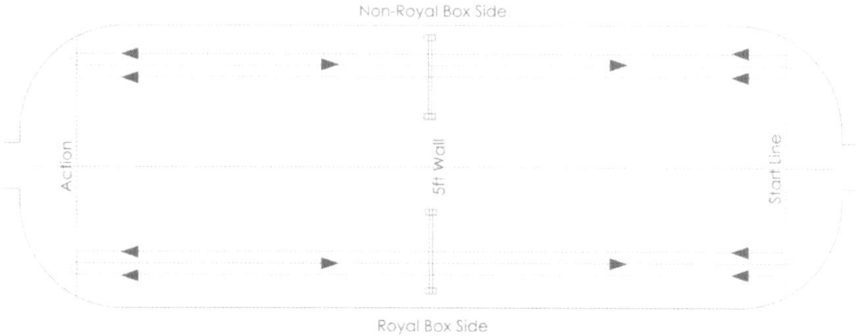

65 - Field Gun Competition layout 1925

The crews went on the action line and fired three rounds. After this "damage is sustained to the gun-carriage and wheels, rendering the gun unworkable and necessitating retirement. The gun wheels, being useless, are left behind, and the gun is taken on out of its carriage and is slung beneath the limber, the damaged carriage being placed on the top". The crew then returned to the wall, crossing over it again and made their way back to the start line.

The programme notes explain that "on arrival at the starting line, it is assumed that a new gun-carriage and wheels are obtained and the gun is again brought into action". The crew then made their way back down the arena, this time passing through the whole in the wall. When they arrived at the action line for a second time, they fired one round, which ended the run. This rather complicated format was only used for one year, the previous format was reinstated in 1926.

An additional 3ft high wall was added to the course in 1928. The crews began in the centre of the arena, crossing the additional wall first with "the gun limbered up i.e. with the gun and limber joined together and going over as one". As before, the crews crossed over the 5 ft walls on the way out and passed through the holes on the way back. They crossed the chasm in both directions. The 3ft wall was removed for the run back to the finish line.

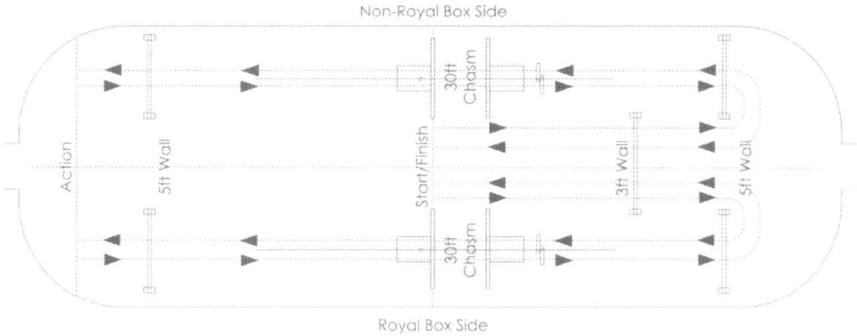

66 - Field Gun Competition layout 1928

The 3ft wall only lasted for one year. The course was amended to a more familiar format in 1929. The programme notes mention bugle calls as part of the competition for the first time (although these are likely to have been used in earlier formats).

From 1929 onwards, the crews began each run on the side of the arena (rather than the centre). Each crew racing down the side of the arena before turning inwards and "encountering their first obstacle a five-foot wall". The programme notes also say that "the are next confronted with a 30-foot-wide chasm, over which guns and men have to be transported on a wire rope" before going over the second wall and bringing the gun into action.

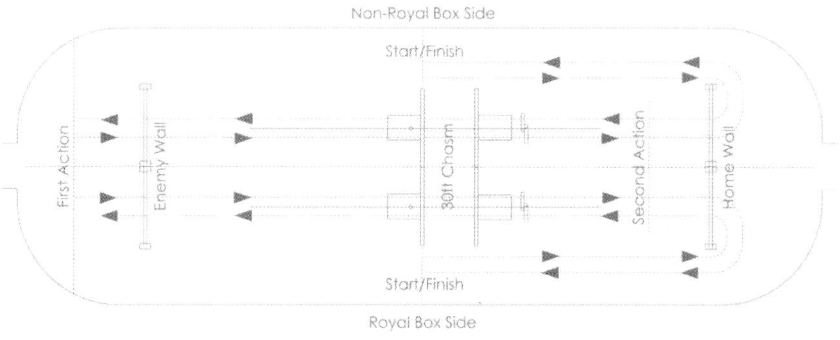

67 - Field Gun Competition layout 1929

The "Retire" was then sounded on the bugle signalling the restart of the competition, the crews passed through the hole in the wall and over the chasm again. After crossing the chasm, the notes say that they "come into action a second time to destroy a further target" before they "finally return through a breach in the first obstacle". The crews finished in line with the Royal Box (on their respective side of the arena).

The programme lists five crews in 1929 H.M.S. Excellent, H.M.S. Victory, H.M.S. Pembroke, H.M.S. Vivid, and Royal Marines. There was another subtle change to the course in 1932, up until this year the crews had gone over both walls on the way out and through the holes in both the walls on the way back. The notes in the 1932 programme say that the crews passed over the first wall and through the second. On the return they did the opposite.

The last crew from the Royal Marines took part in 1934, they were replaced by a Stokers Crew in 1935. There was no Field Gun Competition in 1936, it is believed that this was due to the Abyssinian Crisis. From 1937 to 1939, six crews competed each year, one crew of seamen and one of stokers from each command (Portsmouth, Devonport, and Chatham).

When the Tournament returned in 1947 following the Second World War, a fourth crew was added from Naval Air Command (Fleet Air Arm). One crew from each command competed in the Competition. The course remained the same for the final years at Olympia.

The arena at Olympia was 74m long by 25m wide with curves in all four corners and entrances at either end. The Earls Court arena was 86m long and 39m wide with a main entrance in the backcloth and two entrances in the Warwick Road end of the arena. The format of the competition remained the same when the Tournament relocated to Earls Court in 1950, although the arena was larger the course dimensions were maintained.

Crews lined up on the sides of the arena in line with the Royal Box, starting on the sound of a thunder flash they raced towards the Warwick Road end. The crew on the Royal Box Side turning left and on the Non-Royal Box Side turning right before passing the crew, gun and limber over the 5ft Home Wall.

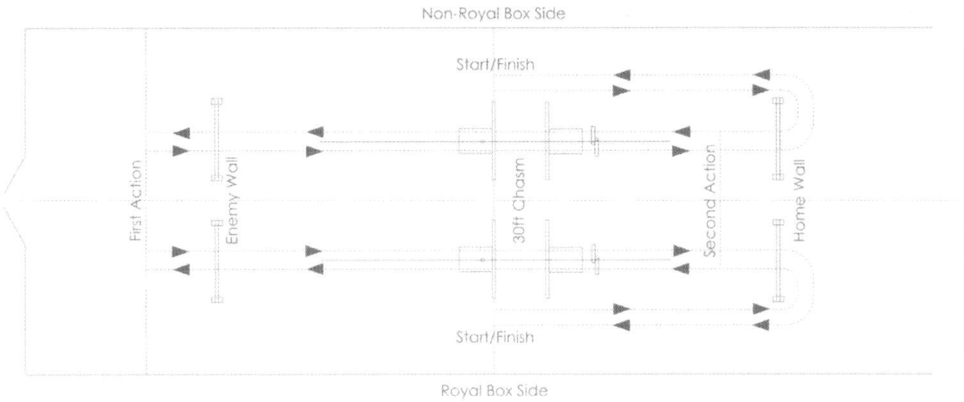

68 - Field Gun Competition layout 1950 (Earls Court)

A pair of sheerlegs and spar were used for the first members of the crew to swing across the 30ft chasm, carrying the wire which was then secured on the enemy side. A 10ft spar was swung across and placed (upright) in the ramp and the wire was placed on top to allow the traveller to be used to bring the rest of the crew and equipment across. Once on the enemy side, the gun and limber along with all 18 crew passed through the 2ft wide hole in the enemy wall. The gun was then brought into action, firing three rounds and the clock was stopped at the end of "The Run Out".

When the crews had reported ready, the Battery Officer gave the signal to restart the run. The Battery Bugler sounded the "Retire" and the crews took their gun and limber over the Enemy Wall and back over the Chasm. As the last man (the flying angel) crossed the chasm, the sheerlegs were collapsed, and the wire was released from the enemy side and was pulled back over to the home side. Each crew then fired a second action (three rounds) in the direction of the enemy, the clock was stopped again at the end of "The Run Back".

The Battery Commander once again gave the signal to restart, the Bugler played the "Cease Fire" and the crews began "The Run Home". They passed through the 2ft wide hole on the Home Wall before hooking up the gun, limber, and drag ropes before turning back down the arena and pulling for home.

The chasm was reduced from 30ft to 28ft in 1957. It is understood that a new 28ft spar (used for the first two members of each crew to swing across the chasm) was introduced in 1957 of laminated construction. There had been issues with equipment failure resulting in penalty points being awarded in previous years. The course then remained the same up until the last run in 1999.

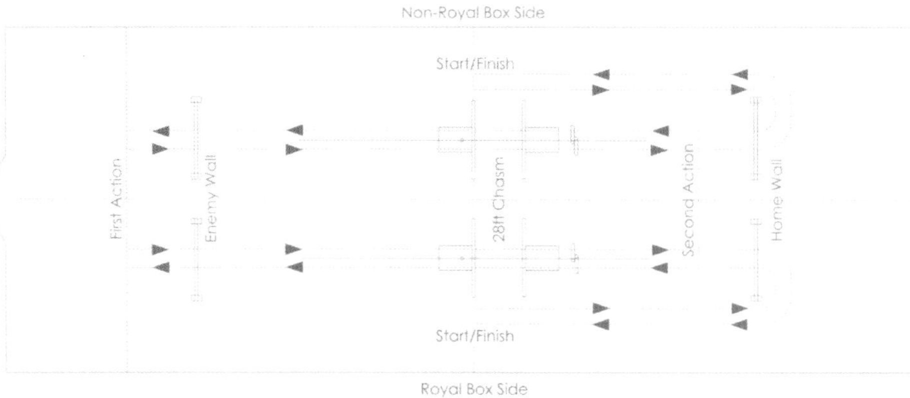

69 - Field Gun Competition layout 1957

Following the 1960 Royal Tournament, Chatham withdrew from the Field Gun Competition, leaving three crews: Portsmouth, Devonport, and Fleet Air Arm to contest the competition until 1999.

The programme notes from 1999 explained the three stages of each run. These notes also formed the basis for the arena commentary by Basil Reitz at Earls Court from 1957 to 1999

"The Run,Out (average time 1 minute 25 seconds)

The guns are raced from the start position down the sides of the arena and manhandled over a 5ft wall. Wooden spars weighing 170lb (77 kilos) are erected and wires rigged across the 28-foot chasm. The first men are hauled across, some carrying 120lb (55 kilos) wheels over their shoulders. The gun carriage and gun barrels follow, the gun barrels each weighing 900lb (409 kilos). The remainder of the crews, wheels and limbers are pulled over the second wall. Each crew then engages the enemy with three rounds.

The Run Back (average time 1 minute)

All the men and gear have to be withdrawn over the wall and back across the chasm. The combined weight of the gun barrel and carriage is 1,250lb (567 kilos); and it goes over in one piece! As soon as the last man of each crew, nicknamed the "Flying Angel", is across the chasm, the rig is collapsed and three rounds are fired in a rearguard action.

The Run Home (average time 21 seconds)

At the sounding of the "G" on the bugle the final phase is to take all their equipment through the narrow gaps in the "Home Wall". In a matter of seconds the wheels are on, pins are in and the crews go racing flat-out to the finishing line.

SELECTED BIBLIOGRAPHY

King, Charles Wallis, THE TOURNAMENT BOOK, Gale & Polden, 1911

Binns, Lieutenant Colonel P.L., THE STORY OF THE ROYAL TOURNAMENT, Gale & Polden Limited, 1952

Chalfont, Lord, THE STORY OF THE ROYAL TOURNAMENT, The Royal Tournament, 1980

Bridgland, Tony, Field Gun Jack Versus the Boers: The Royal Navy in South Africa 1899-1900, Pen & Sword, 1998, ISBN-13: 9780850525809

Glanfield, John, FROM BUFFALO BILL TO THE 'BRITS', Sutton Publishing Ltd, 2003, ISBN 0 7509 2998 7

Forshaw, Alec, THE BUILDING THAT LIVED TWICE, Business Design Centre, 2011, ISBN-13: 978-0-9541490-3-1

Parker, Micheal, IT'S ALL GOING TERRIBLY WRONG, THE ACCIDENTAL SHOWMAN, Bene Factum Publishing Ltd, 2012, ISBN 978-1-903071-65-6

Parker, Micheal, IMAGES OF THE ROYAL TOURNAMENT 1974 – 1999, 2017

INDEX

With a little help from our friends…

There are many people who have, in one way or another, helped me on the journey of writing this book, in more recent years or in the past. Below are the names of a few (apologies to any that I have missed).

Brig. Robin Bacon
Victor Barnett
Stuart Baynes
Capt. Adrian Beckett
Mike Bell
Catie Bland
Mike Boxall
Katherine Browne
Brian Browne
Julian Carmichael
Jane Charley
John Chiverton
Sophie Coad
Michael Dewey
Angela Donaldson
Maj. George Douglas
Kate Eastwood
David Edwards
Sarah Elton-Wall
Col. Iain Ferguson
Maj. David Hammond
Des Hart
Tony Hawkins
Janine Hislop
Terry Hissey
Lt. Col. Alec Jackson
Christopher Joll
Angelique Kelly
Ruby Kerrison
Keegan Leon
Jo Lester
Sgt Ian Liptrott
Joanne Mathias
Nick Mattingley
Lt. Col Ian Mckenzie
Brian Meadows
Harriet Nelson
Maj. Sir Micheal Parker
Lady Emma Parker
Lynne Parsons
Suzie Pollock
Alan Purdie
Basil Reitz
Capt. Chris Sayer
Claire Sheppard
Heidi Sheppard
Jarrod Steadman
Clarinda Tompkin
Kate Vandenburg
Maj. Gen Sir Evelyn Webb-Carter
Dave Whymark
Skye Wood
Brian Young
Valarie Young

ABOUT THE AUTHOR

The family tradition of visiting the Royal Tournament had been established long before Roger was born. His Great Grandfather had served in the Grenadier Guards during the Great War, Roger's Grandmother recalled being taken to Olympia in the 1920s and 1930s to see the Tournament. She along with her children, grandchildren, and great grandchildren visited the Tournament up until the Last Run in 1999.

Roger first visited the Tournament in 1979, aged two. The trip to London to see the show each year soon became the highlight of the summer. He began making working models of the Tournament Backcloths and would send photographs of the models to the Producer, who kindly wrote back each year! In 1994, Roger began volunteering in the Press Office of the Tournament, supporting the Royal Tournament Brigade. Initially manning the Brigade Stand at the show and later writing the Brigade Newsletters. In the final year of the Tournament, he also supported the Tug of War Competition in the Earls Court Arena.

Following the Last Run in 1999, Roger was invited to join the team responsible for delivering the Royal Military Tattoo 2000 (RMT2000). He worked with the front of house team, managing the Usher Control Room on Horseguards Parade for both RMT2000 and the Queen Mothers 100th Birthday Celebrations.

He setup the RoyalTournament.org website in 2005 to keep alive the memory of the Tournament. During 2008, he was approached by Maj. Gen. Sir Evelyn Webb-Carter and was invited to join the team who went on to deliver the British Military Tournament at Earls Court from 2010-2013.

Roger has produced a wide range of events during his career including the H.M.S. Victory 250th Anniversary Concert, Fort Nelson Tattoo, Portsmouth VE-DAY 70th Anniversary Concert, as well as concerts with the Band of HM Royal Marines, RAF Squadronaires, and The Band of the Royal Artillery. In October 2024, he produced the Royal Tournament 25th Anniversary Concert with The Band of the Royal Yeomanry.

Printed in Great Britain
by Amazon

61675547R00130